creating
a positive
self-image

Ursula Markham is a practising hypnotherapist and business training provider. In addition to running her own successful clinic, she gives lectures and conducts workshops and seminars in Britain and abroad. She has appeared frequently on radio and television and is Principal of the *Hypnothink Foundation*, which is responsible for the training of hypnotherapists and counsellors to professional level.

creating
a positive
self-image

simple techniques to transform your life

ursula markham

First published by Element Books Ltd 1995
© Vega 2002
Text © Ursula Markham 1995

COVER DESIGN **Balley Design Associates**

ISBN 1-84333-598-0

A catalogue record for this book is
available from the British Library

Published in 2002 by
Vega
64 Brewery Road
London, N7 9NT

A member of **Chrysalis** Books plc

Visit our website at **www.chrysalisbooks.co.uk**

PRINTED IN GREAT BRITAIN
BY CREATIVE PRINT AND DESIGN (WALES), EBBW VALE

Contents

To my mother and sons
with love

Hos successus alit; possunt, quia posse videntur.
These success encourages; they can because they think they can.

Virgil, *Aeneid*, Book 5.

Introduction

In 1974, just when he was achieving his greatest successes in the theatre and on BBC television, Romark, the famous mentalist – whose technique involves concentrated use of the brain to perform amazing feats of mental agility – suffered a massive stroke. He was in London, having recently completed long runs of his one-man show in Hollywood and South Africa. Instead of taking the time to relax, he had embarked on a round of radio and television interviews and cabaret performances – all of which finally took their toll in the form of the stroke. Romark was rushed to the intensive care unit of a major London hospital unable to speak or move. The prognosis of his consultants was short and to the point: 'This man will never work again.'

By using a technique he later called Hypnothink, Romark did not simply recover his speech and his mobility: just eight weeks later he appeared on Jimmy Savile's *Clunk Click* television programme where he once again demonstrated his skills as a master mentalist.

Now that same technique is available for you to use to create a better and more positive self-image. Using Hypnothink you can learn to re-programme your mind and rearrange your life, just as Romark did, so that you can achieve success in whatever area of your life you choose.

Your self-image is vitally important. The way you feel about yourself affects everything you say and do. It influences your state of health and your relationships. The more positive your self-image, the more you will be able to create for yourself the kind of life you truly desire. When obstacles present themselves, you will have the strength of purpose to overcome them; when all is going well, you will have sufficient confidence to enjoy it; and, most important of all, you will at last be in control of your own life.

Creating a more positive self-image will be easier than you think. So start now and learn to become the person you have always wanted to be.

1

Create a better self-image with Hypnothink

R omark had more than one career. As well as being a world-famous mentalist he was also a clinical hypnotherapist. When not involved in touring the world giving performances of his one-man show, he would see individual patients in his London consulting rooms, helping them to overcome a diversity of problems. He was therefore familiar with the way in which the subconscious mind can be employed to help us alter our thought patterns and the actions which result from them.

Lying in his hospital bed, unable to move, Romark had nothing to use to help himself except the power of his own mind. For the first time in many years he had nothing to do but think – and plenty of time to do it in. He thought about the events which had led up to his illness and it came to him that every human being has the ability within himself to mould his future to a far more precise degree than is commonly imagined.

The human mind has amazing powers – a fact which is being accepted more and more widely in the most respected medical and scientific quarters. The threshold of the mind is probably the most exciting frontier we have yet attempted to cross.

Romark had time to think of the significance of his experiences with hypnosis and suggestion – with the programming of the thought processes. He realized that success, once achieved, provided the springboard for further successes. As someone who frequented the world of sportsmen and women, he reflected on the procedure sometimes followed by trainers who are preparing a promising boxer for future triumphs. In order to bolster the aspiring boxer's confidence, it is not unknown for a victory to be 'arranged'. Whatever the ethics of this practice, having become convinced that he is able to succeed, the boxer will usually go on to do so on his own ability.

At this point Romark reached the conclusion which lies at the very heart of Hypnothink: the successes which are necessary to programme people for even greater things need only take place in the imagination.

Romark wrote several books on various aspects of using the mind to improve one's life. When describing how Hypnothink had helped him to reprogramme his own life, changing potential disaster into triumph, he wrote:

> When I was in hospital after the stroke they wanted me to use a bedpan, but I didn't like the idea. I decided to use the toilet in the normal way. But I was paralysed. I couldn't walk.
>
> I decided to employ that theory which I had recently developed. I changed my self-image. To put it another way – I altered my Inner Face.
>
> I knew for a fact that I was paralysed and couldn't walk. But I forced myself to imagine that I could walk as far as the toilet. I pictured myself walking as far as the toilet and I convinced myself that I had, in fact, walked to the toilet.
>
> I did this step by step – a laborious process. I didn't just imagine in general terms that I got up and went to the toilet. I pictured in my mind's eye every single detail, every move involved in the whole trip. And I expended on the thought process the same amount of time which would have been taken by the actual physical actions that I was visualizing.
>
> I hadn't actually done it yet, so the action I contemplated – and which I saw so clearly in my mind – still lay in the future.
>
> Finally I convinced myself – still within my imagination – that I had actually made the trip to the toilet and returned to my hospital bed.
>
> I repeated this mental process numerous times a day over

a period of several days – remember I had very little else to do – and, at the end of that time, I got up out of bed, walked to the toilet and came back to bed once more. The nurses, of course, were amazed.

I had succeeded in converting the future to the present tense. I had employed a form of hypnosis without resorting to the customary trance-state. I had been 'un-hypnotized' throughout.

If anyone reading these words thinks that a similar feat is beyond his capabilities, let me point out that the principle involved is precisely the same as the one by which countless people 'programme' themselves to wake up at a particular time in the morning without the help of an alarm clock.

Each person is capable of programming himself to achieve his or her aims.

I had had a stroke because of my own foolishness. My life-style was all wrong. I had been overworking for a long time – mainly because I was on an ego trip. In Durban I had broken the record for the longest-running one-man show in world theatre history. That was an ego trip if ever there was one!

Breaking that record had been an extraordinarily difficult feat due to the sheer physical strain involved – 1080 hours on stage. It was a one-man show. I was on stage uninterruptedly for every performance lasting over three hours.

I had suffered from a heart condition since childhood and the specialists who examined me after the stroke established that, by subjecting myself to the strain involved in breaking the world record, I had weakened my heart still further.

Then, after leaving Africa, I had gone to the United States where I gave fourteen performances a week instead of the customary six.

I was doing too much in too short a time. My lifestyle had become so intense and high-pressured that it would inevitably have killed me.

We all recognize that these pressures are all too common in our modern society. The rat race is taking its toll to an ever-increasing degree. Human beings were never intended to live this way. That is why more and more people, particularly business people in high-pressure occupations, are having strokes and heart attacks.

A stroke is caused by a clot of blood detaching itself from the walls of the main artery, travelling to the brain and damaging cells there. In a large percentage of cases this causes instant death. In many others the victim is extensively paralysed – even to the extent of becoming a 'human vegetable'. Some, through the use of extensive physiotherapy, make a partial recovery. It is very rare indeed for a serious stroke not to leave a visible and permanent trace in the victim.

Eight weeks to the day after having his stroke, Romark was a guest star on Jimmy Savile's television show. He carried out an experiment which required a great deal of concentration on his part – and it was a complete success. As he later wrote:

> I did this with Hypnothink. It was just a continuation of that thought process by which I made myself walk to the toilet when I was paralysed.

The technique of Hypnothink which Romark used to such great effect involved changing his self-image from that of someone who was paralysed to that of someone who could walk if he wanted to. That is a far more extreme example than most people are likely to encounter. But if it works for something as dramatic as paralysis, it is going to work equally well for all those other negative thoughts with which our minds are so often filled.

Your self-image – or, as Romark termed it, your Inner Face – governs the way you act and react in all situations in life. At one time people believed that you could not change this inner image of yourself and therefore you would be compelled to go on acting in the same way throughout your life. We now know, however, that this Inner Face is something which can be changed – and I believe that Hypnothink is the most effective way of doing so.

In the years that followed his recovery, Romark went on to use the technique of Hypnothink to help many other people overcome their problems. One of the people he helped was the actress Shirley Jones who was at the time starring (with her stepson David Cassidy) in the television series *The Partridge Family*. Shirley Jones was so delighted at the way Hypnothink worked for her that she gave Romark express permission to use her name in the hope that it might encourage other people to gain similar advantages.

An entire new series for television had just been written and Shirley Jones was to be one of the stars. The plot was to take place aboard an ocean liner on its way to Acapulco. To most of us this would appear to be a delightful setting in which to work. But when Shirley Jones read the first script she began to panic. For years she had suffered from a phobia about travel and she saw no way in which she could go on a boat. There seemed to be no alternative – she would have to turn the series down.

But she asked Romark if he could help her. He taught her Hypnothink – and she was cured. Not only did she make that television series on the ship but at the end of it she threw a party for Romark to thank him for making it all possible.

She had been helped to change her Inner Face. Instead of seeing herself as someone who positively cringed from the prospect of travel, who thought of herself as insecure, unsafe and threatened aboard a ship, she learned to see herself as a person radiantly happy at the prospect of a sea voyage – a woman enjoying everything an ocean trip had to offer.

She had programmed her own computer – her mind – and had succeeded in creating for herself the image she really wanted.

HOW DOES HYPNOTHINK WORK?

As human beings, we inherit certain genetic characteristics from our parents, such as the colour of our eyes and other aspects of our physical make-up. But mentally we begin life rather like an empty computer. As we grow up, information is fed into the memory cells of that computer – our mind – and this gradually creates the inner image on which we base our actions and behaviour.

We have all seen that animals inherit certain instincts. When a sheepdog is still a puppy, for example, it will herd chickens together in a farmyard although it has never been taught to do so. It is a purely instinctive action.

In the same way, homing pigeons find their way back to their lofts over distances of hundreds of miles and through the worst weather conditions without ever having been taught to do so.

I believe that the first instinct which is firmly implanted in the human make-up is the inclination to survive, and the second is the inclination to *succeed*. People love to succeed.

In the early part of our life we receive an in-flow of information which creates certain patterns of behaviour – ways in which we react to certain situations. But habit-patterns can be imposed on creatures in a planned way. This was clearly demonstrated by the Russian scientist Pavlov with his experiments in which he caused dogs to salivate at the sound of a tinkling bell instead of when they received food.

In the same way it is possible for human beings to 'programme' themselves – just as a computer is programmed. Programming is not as unlikely as it sounds. Many people have programmed themselves at some time or other to wake up early in the morning for an important appointment. One of the most commonly used techniques is to bang your head on the pillow the required number of times – seven times for seven o'clock in the morning, for example. A very simple concept – but one which enables you to programme yourself for anything.

A research programme carried out at Stanford University in the United States established that the mind is at its most receptive to this sort of suggestion programme at two periods of the day – just before waking in the

morning and just before going t⟨
isn't really feasible for most of us
sleep-learning mechanisms for thε
of receptivity, we need to make ⟨
before going to sleep. This, then,
practising the Hypnothink techni⟨
learn in this book.

WHY HYPNOTHINK?

You have already decided that you want to improve your
life and to change your self-image – and Hypnothink is
one of the quickest methods of doing so. You are likely
to see beneficial results in a relatively short time – even
if achieving your final goal takes longer. And, of course,
as soon as you become aware of some improvement, you
grow happier, pleased with yourself and confident in your
ability to make those changes. Your increased sense of
positivity and the reassurance that Hypnothink is a valid
technique make the following stages even easier and more
likely to show even quicker results.

This doesn't mean that you don't have to make some
effort if you are to be successful. Hypnothink works – but
only if you work at it! It may only take fifteen minutes a
day to deal with most situations – but that means fifteen
minutes *every single day*. However, if you know that you
are going to be able to turn your life around in some
satisfactory way, it has to be worth going to sleep fifteen
minutes later than usual if that is the only quiet time you
can find.

Many aspects of orthodox medicine involve looking at
and attempting to cure symptoms rather than people.
You may consult a doctor because you have an injured
arm, suffer from insomnia, are terrified of beetles or
have backache. And all but the most forward-thinking of
doctors will simply bandage your arm, give you sleeping
pills, or prescribe something to 'calm you down' or rub

back. None of these is a bad thing in the short
but unless the underlying cause is dealt with, the
e problem or a similar one is likely to recur.

Hypnothink is a truly holistic concept. Because it
involves physical relaxation as well as positive use of
the imagination and the emotions, it works towards
healing the whole person rather than just one aspect.
And because the various parts of any individual are so
strongly interrelated, you will find that overcoming one
problem will automatically help you to feel better in many
other ways, too. As soon as you start to use Hypnothink,
you will begin to have more faith in yourself and your
abilities. You will know that you are starting to exercise
real control over your life.

You do not have to suffer from a physical or psychological problem in order to benefit from Hypnothink. In
fact, one area where it is highly effective is the world
of sport. Naturally, using the technique cannot replace
the training, practice and sheer hard work which goes
into any fitness regime. But by using Hypnothink it is
possible for any sports person to play to the best of his
or her ability.

Notice I have said 'to the best of his or her ability',
which is not the same as guaranteeing that he or she will
win. This is because two sprinters in the same race could
practise Hypnothink on a regular basis but of course only
one can win. This will be the one who is fitter or faster
than the other. But even the one who does not win will
be likely to give the best performance of his or her life.

When dealing with teams, however, an actual win
becomes far more likely. If you have a number of people –
whether it is seven, eleven or fifteen – each playing to the
best of their ability, they are almost bound to win. Take
any team on any given day and you will find that there are
several problem areas. One player may be feeling a little
tired, another may have money problems; one may have
had a row with his partner while another may have been
made redundant. Whatever the reasons, you are likely to

find that at least two will be playing under par – and this is sufficient to jeopardize the performance of the entire team. But, whatever the problems, if each individual member has programmed himself for success, the team will be almost invincible.

Some sportspeople have been using a type of Hypnothink for years – particularly those trained in the United States or the former Soviet Union, where there has long been an awareness of the importance of psychological as well as physical preparation. As far back as 1974, at the Wimbledon tennis championships, you could see the defending champion Jimmy Connors doing his best to programme his mind for success.

Connors' procedure was to place one ball in his pocket in case of a fault and bounce the other three times before throwing it in the air for the service. He never departed from this ritual. Once he was distracted by a ball-boy as he was going through that ritual bouncing. Connors stopped and began the whole procedure all over again: three bounces, throw the ball in the air and then serve. Possibly he had done this on one occasion and won the important match of a lifetime. Whatever the original reason, Connors believed that if he had been prevented from bouncing the ball three times, his playing pattern would have been so disrupted that he might have been eliminated from that year's competition.

HOW CAN HYPNOTHINK HELP?

Let's look now at how Hypnothink can help someone who does have a specific problem to overcome.

Sandra had a phobia about water. She did not know when or how it had started – and the original cause did not really bother her. All she was concerned with was putting an end to a situation which was becoming more and more difficult to live with.

You might think that a water phobia is not such a

terrible thing. After all, you can live your life without swimming or going on a boat. And, indeed, these had been Sandra's original fears. But any phobia which is not dealt with in the early stages will always grow more intense. Because a phobia is by definition 'an illogical fear', the sufferer will be very conscious of the illogicality of it and the fact that it makes him or her different from everyone else. This will lower their self-esteem and, as a result of negative emotions feeding upon a poor self-image, they will become more disgusted with themselves and more ashamed of their behaviour. They will therefore spend a greater proportion of their time thinking about themselves, their inadequacies and their phobia – and this in turn will develop and grow.

From being a teenager with a fear of swimming and boats – although for no reason she could bring to mind – Sandra became a young woman who would cross the road to avoid puddles after a shower of rain and would not even go out of the house if there was a particularly violent rainstorm. As the years passed, her phobia increased until she was unable to go out in the rain at all. She then developed a phobia about having a bath or a shower in her own home. What finally brought her to see me was a growing dislike of putting her hands in water in order to have a wash.

So, while it might be quite possible to live well and happily without plunging into the sea, by the time you reach the stage of being frightened of washing your hands your whole life is dramatically affected.

I shall come back later in this book to show you precisely how Sandra overcame her phobia with Hypnothink, but for the moment it is sufficient to understand that problems have to be dealt with one step at a time. The first thing I worked on with Sandra was turning on the taps of the handbasin in her bathroom and letting the water run over her fingers. This she was able to do after just one session and a few more days of practice. That might seem a very trivial achievement to you if you have never had a horror of water, but to Sandra it was a glorious success and a step in the right direction. Because it gave her confidence in Hypnothink, and her ability to use it, she *knew* that she was going to reverse the progress of her phobia and eventually eliminate it altogether.

After that initial success, Sandra told me that she did not mind how long it took to rid her of her water phobia because she was convinced that it would work in the end. But I told you Hypnothink was a speedy process, and after just seven weeks Sandra was able to take a bath, go out in the rain and even step in puddles. She still had no desire to go sailing or learn to swim, but the terror of doing so had vanished, having been replaced by a lack of desire, and she felt that she could live quite happily with this situation.

Although Hypnothink can help you in many areas of your life there are, of course, things it cannot do. It cannot cure a problem which is *only* physical. A broken leg is a broken leg and will take however long a broken leg takes to heal. Having said that, because of the holistic nature of Hypnothink, I am convinced that it can speed the healing process by helping you to become more positive and less stressed about the situation.

Some problems which appear to be of physical origin have an underlying emotional cause and here, even if it does not bring about a total cure, Hypnothink can play a significant role. From headaches to psoriasis, from pre-menstrual tension to some forms of cancer, many conditions which demonstrate physical symptoms either result from or are exacerbated by emotional distress. In a great number of these cases Hypnothink can help to alleviate – and sometimes dispel – symptoms and discourage their reoccurrence.

But people suffering the after-effects of a dramatic and distressing trauma, or with a history of chronic depression, really need the benefit of a professional counsellor or therapist to help them overcome their problems. Because of their negative state of mind – which may not be their fault – they would find it too difficult to create the dedication and positive effort needed for Hypnothink to work.

Because concentration and a certain amount of effort are required if the technique is to prove effective, young children and those who are unable, for whatever reason, to fully understand what Hypnothink entails or to sustain their level of concentration would be less likely to benefit from using the method.

WHO CAN HYPNOTHINK HELP?

We've looked at who is not likely to find Hypnothink particularly helpful – but who is the ideal subject? Who is the person likely to gain speedy and long-lasting benefit from this way of harnessing the mind's precious power? The answer is – YOU! You are just the right sort of person – the one who will be able to change their life, attain their goals and achieve success with Hypnothink.

How do I know this? The first essentials are:

- to realize that change is necessary
- to want that change to come about
- to be willing to put in some effort to make it happen

All those three things apply to you, don't they? After all, you chose to read this book in the first place. Therefore you must realize that some change is necessary and you must want it to come about. You have already passed the passage which told you that you are going to have to work at making it happen – and you are still reading. Therefore you must be willing to put in the required effort to bring about those changes. So you are the ideal person to benefit from the technique of Hypnothink – and this book is going to show you how.

2

Who are you?

Do you know who you are? You're probably thinking to yourself that that's a daft question – but is it? How do we form opinions about ourselves? Often it is by comparing ourselves to other people or by listening to the views and comments of those we know. But is this really the ideal way to discover the true you?

DISCOVERING THE REAL YOU

Letting your opinion of yourself be formed – directly or indirectly – by the views of other people is rather like looking in the mirror and hoping to see yourself as you really appear. This, of course is impossible. The one thing you do not see when you look in the mirror is a true image of yourself. Everything is reversed – left is where right should be and vice versa. What you see is your mirror image and not what you really look like.

At the fairground you can find mirrors which deliberately distort the image and make you appear long and thin, short and squat or peculiarly shaped. You do not believe that these images depict the real you. And yet we often form our opinion of ourselves because of things said or done by people who start from a distorted viewpoint. Some of these people are deliberately malicious, but most simply do not know or understand us well enough to be accurate. So it cannot be sensible to judge ourselves by their comments or ideals.

Until you fully understand the point from which you are starting, it is very difficult to formulate a plan which will enable you to make deliberate changes in yourself. Many of us fool ourselves about our personalities – being hypercritical or painting an exceptionally glowing picture depending on whether we are in a negative or positive mood at the time. But unless you begin from a position of self-understanding, any changes you might make will be a somewhat hit or miss affair.

Those who are insecure and lacking in confidence might well have learned to put on quite a convincing act so that other people believe them to be far more self-assured than they really are. Others who are quite calm and capable but don't make a fuss about their achievements may be perceived by others as being less able than they in fact are. Only the individual concerned knows the truth and it is only on this self-knowledge that future success can be built.

Pigeon-holing

Most people are guilty, to a greater or lesser extent, of 'pigeon-holing' others – casting them in a certain mould from which they are never allowed to escape. They are then treated in a way which conforms with this initial classification, and even if they make some dramatic change in themselves, this is how they are likely to go on being thought of.

Bill never did very well at school in the early years. He wasn't unintelligent but seemed to find concentration difficult and, when asked a question, would sometimes sit there, just staring into space. Eventually he was put in a pigeon-hole by everyone. His teachers considered that he was not very bright and tended to leave him alone when asking questions of the class. The other children in his group laughed at him when he did not seem to understand what was going on. The crueller ones called him names and made fun of him. Even his own parents tended to think he was 'not as bright as our other children'. And although they never said such a thing in front of Bill, the thought was obviously apparent from the atmosphere at home.

When Bill was nine it was discovered that he was slightly deaf. The deficiency in his hearing was not enough to cause him problems in one-to-one situations, but it did make it difficult for him to understand everything said in the classroom or when there was a group of people chatting and making noise around him. Bill himself had never realized that he had a hearing problem – after all, he had nothing to act as a standard so did not know that he was in any way different from anyone else.

By means of a tiny hearing aid in one ear, Bill's hearing ability was brought up to a satisfactory level and he was at last able to follow what went on during lessons. However, this did not bring about the 'happy ending' you might have expected. For one thing, Bill had a lot of catching up to do as his earlier lack of understanding of what was being said had caused him to fall behind in his work. But a far bigger hurdle was the way he was seen in everyone else's eyes. Teachers and pupils alike were so used to thinking of Bill as someone not very bright that they tended to continue doing so and treated him accordingly. It was only when, at the age of eleven, Bill changed schools that he was able to start again and be accepted for what he was by those around him.

In just the same way, if someone once told you that you were untalented – and if this was someone who you chose at the time to believe – that is how you will have learned to think of yourself. But that is not the same as saying that you really *are* untalented.

UNDERSTANDING YOUR INNER FACE

So, before you can go ahead and discover how you can change yourself with Hypnothink, you need to learn about the person you really are at the moment. You need to understand what we call the Inner Face. This is another way of describing your mind, your mental attitudes, your unique combination of personality, values and individual characteristics as you yourself see them. The trouble is that some people have an extremely distorted Inner Face – in either a negative or a positive way.

Some people with a negative Inner Face will act out their imagined inferiority and will even wish (subconsciously) to retain it. The man who says that he is an unsuccessful salesman will actually create circumstances which make it difficult for him to sell – even to a willing buyer. He is so used to his Inner Face as a poor salesman that to become successful would prove uncomfortable.

Any plastic surgeon can cite countless examples of people who have had totally successful cosmetic operations which have not succeeded in bringing about the desired personality change. The 'ugly duckling' may have undergone a dramatic physical transformation but he or she has grown so used to thinking of themselves as 'odd', 'ugly' or 'different' that this is what they continue to do.

Ask any anorexic what she sees when she looks in the mirror and she will tell you that she sees someone fat and unattractive. And because anorexia arises as a result of a massive sense of inferiority, this is what she really does see – even if to everyone else she looks little more than skin and bone.

Janette was a leading photographic model in the United States. One day a photographer told her that although her figure was perfect and her eyes beautiful, he found her nose a little too broad at the bridge. 'Without that,' he said 'you would be perfect.'

Those few words of somewhat flippant criticism became an obsession with Janette. Her friends considered this a harmless and slightly amusing personality foible, but the shape of her nose played more and more on Janette's mind. One day she obtained a small role in a film and, as filming progressed, she became a close friend of the leading man. She told him of her longing to have the perfect nose. His generous reaction was to say, 'If you want the perfect nose, you shall have the perfect nose.' He took her to a leading plastic surgeon and she went into hospital to have an operation to alter the shape of her nose.

Immediately after the operation, as is usually the case, Janette felt most uncomfortable. Her face was black and blue as though she had been attacked and beaten up. Within a few weeks, however, the swelling and bruising disappeared and her new nose could be seen in all its glory. It was the shape of nose she had personally selected from the various shapes offered to her by the plastic surgeon.

When her friends saw Janette with her new nose they were, in fact, rather disappointed. Its beautiful symmetry seemed to have been destroyed and its character removed.

The change in Janette herself, however, was remarkable. Her eyes blazed with new-found confidence; she spoke with fire and eloquence. In her own eyes – in her Inner Face – she had become the ultimate beauty. When one or two of her friends mentioned that they preferred the shape of her nose as it had been before the operation, she just laughed.

Janette may have acquired an inferior nose on her outer face but she had given herself an impeccable, new Inner Face. She went on to become happy and extremely successful in her modelling career and later in films.

How your Inner Face affects you

So many things can influence your Inner Face and the way you feel about yourself. We have already seen how other people can have caused you to form opinions about yourself which may be distorted. Various aspects of the media can also affect how you see yourself. The heroes and heroines in plays, films and on television are for the most part beautiful people with lovely faces and slender bodies. But as Joan Collins once commented in an interview when complimented on her enduring good looks, 'Don't think I wake up in the morning looking like this!' These people work hard to achieve the image they portray. It isn't real life – but if you want to enjoy a good play or film, you don't necessarily want to sit and watch 'real life'; there is a lot to be said for some make-believe escapism – it is much more pleasurable to see. If any of you ever enjoy a good cry, you must wonder how the leading ladies manage to look so beautiful when they weep – while the rest of us just get red, puffy and blotchy!

Of course we all know that there is a difference between what we see on stage or screen and reality, but the insidiousness of the subconscious message still persists. Somewhere deep inside is a little voice wondering why you cannot be as capable, beautiful, exciting and sexy as the man or woman brought by television into your home. And to all those who say that we are not influenced at all by what we see on our television screens, perhaps they would explain why advertisers spend so many hundreds of thousands of pounds trying to do just that.

YOUR OUTER FACE AND INNER/OUTER FACE

As well as an Inner Face, we have an Outer Face which is the way other people see us. We also have an Inner/Outer Face. This is the way we *think* other people see us – not necessarily the same thing at all.

When Diane was promoted to Head of Department she

was naturally delighted. She was bright, efficient and a hard worker, and had no doubt that she could do the job well. What did cause her some problems was that she was being promoted over the heads of people who were older than she was and who had been with the company for longer. This created in her a sense of embarrassment which she tried to hide from the members of her team.

As it happened, no one in the department resented Diane's promotion. They recognized her abilities and her dedication to the job and were quite happy with the situation. But what they did resent was her change in attitude.

To cover her nervousness and her embarrassment at the situation which had arisen, Diane had decided to maintain an air of cool efficiency in place of the somewhat jollier camaraderie which had previously existed. Her colleagues, however, mistook this for an indication that Diane was feeling superior to them; they thought that she was acting in a conceited fashion and reacted accordingly.

So here was a conflict between Diane's Outer Face (the way others saw her), which was as an arrogant and distant person, and her Inner/Outer Face (the way she thought they saw her), which was as a calm and competent leader of the department.

MAKING THE MOST OF YOUR LIFE

Before you can get Hypnothink to work efficiently for you, it is necessary to link up your Inner, Outer and Inner/Outer Faces so that you get as true a picture as possible – which often necessitates getting help from someone close to you. Later in this chapter you will find a step-by-step method for achieving this.

By using an efficient self-help technique to improve

your life in whatever way you believe to be most appropriate, you may also be helping yourself to progress along your personal path of evolvement. Whatever your religious belief – or even if you have none at all – I'm sure you accept that there is more than just the here and now. You may believe that we have only one life, or you may feel that we live many times. Whatever the case, it must be right for us to work to develop and evolve as we strive to improve ourselves.

My own belief is that each individual spirit journeys through many lifetimes, having chosen different lessons to learn during the course of each one. I do not, however, believe in absolute predestination; we are not simply puppets having our strings pulled by some giant unknown force. You and I – the human beings within whom these spirits temporarily live – have to make our decisions. When choices arise, we are the ones who have to select the type of behaviour we wish to display or the path we wish to follow. Depending upon the choices we make, we either go forward on our spiritual journey or we do not.

But even if I am wrong – even if we are each here for one lifetime only – it is still up to us to make the most of that life and to try to become better people. Of course, we will make mistakes along the way, but an error is simply part of the learning process. Without doing something wrong, we would have no way of knowing what was right.

And nothing will come of simply sitting back and waiting for it to happen. I have known people who have insisted that God (or Spirit or Fate) will provide and who have gone home and waited for something wonderful to occur. I have had patients who have consulted me as a hypnotherapist and asked me to *make* something happen – which of course I cannot do. I have no magic wand to wave over them. What I can do is help them to help themselves in whatever way they wish; but they have to put in a good deal of hard work, too. Using Hypnothink you can learn to change your life and your future – but you are also going to have to make some effort in order to achieve this.

EVALUATING YOUR DIFFERENT FACES

The first thing is to evaluate your different Faces – and this is how you do it:

Inner Face

This is the one you are going to be working on as you make those changes, but before you can begin you need to understand the difference between your own view of yourself and that of other people.

There is plenty of self-deception with Inner Faces. That is why, if you want to benefit from Hypnothink, it is essential that you evaluate yourself meticulously and try to see your true Inner Face. Be very critical – but be honest.

Of course, some people are so paranoid that they put all the blame for their faults onto others. Such people can never get a clear picture of themselves. They would need professional help to reach a stage of accurate self-evaluation.

Start by making a list of all the things about yourself that you like and all those that you do not. Stick to those aspects which are capable of being changed – if you are unhappy with the length of your nose or the size of your feet there is not a great deal you can do about it by means of Hypnothink.

It is best to compile these lists over a period of several days or the length of each will depend upon how positive or negative you feel at a particular moment. And remember – this is only how *you* see yourself, not how someone else tells you that you are.

There is no virtue in having a great, long list of 'dislikes' and only a couple of items in the 'likes' column. I am not asking you to be modest any more than I would wish you to be over-vain. But it is a fact that we are brought up to think more about the negative aspects of ourselves than the positive ones, and because of this there are likely to be more items on the list of aspects you do not like.

It is also all too easy to fall into the trap of summarizing a positive attribute in a single word, but turning a negative one into several items. For example, 'shy', 'nervous with strangers' and 'not very good in large groups' are really different ways of saying the same thing.

Let's have a look at the Inner Face profile compiled by someone I worked with some time ago (I'll call her Margot). Margot came to see me because she was suffering a confidence crisis in both her personal and her working life. She felt that she was being put upon by her boss and her immediate superiors in the office and that she was not being well treated by her boyfriend, Tony. The first time I saw her, her Inner Face lists looked like this:

Likes: *Dislikes:*

Caring   Timid
Helpful   Weak
            No confidence
            Shy
            Not assertive enough
            Foolish
            Can't say no
            Miserable – cries too often

At first glance it might appear that Margot had far more dislikes than likes – but is this really the case? Many of those items can be grouped. 'Weak', 'timid', 'no confidence', 'shy', 'not assertive enough ' and 'can't say no' are all part of the same thing. So the list can be shortened immediately.

Inner/Outer Face

Once you have completed your Inner Face Profile, it is time to make another list. This time, write down how you think other people perceive you. Once again be honest with yourself.

Margot's list read as follows:

How other people see me:

Nervous
Inefficient
Shy
Useless
No fun to have around
Boring

Here you could group together 'nervous' and 'shy' – also, 'no fun to have around' and 'boring'.

Outer Face

To compile your Outer Face profile you need to enlist the help of one or more other people. Be sure these are people you can trust to give you a fair and honest opinion. False praise may be very flattering in the short term but will not help you to build up a fair picture of yourself. Ask each of these people to list as many of your characteristics (positive and negative) as they can.

For this part of the exercise, Margot enlisted the help of two people – her younger sister, to whom she was quite close, and a woman who worked in her office. Her sister's list read:

Kind
Helpful
Clever

Not very good at standing up for herself
Over-protective when we were young
Expects too much of herself

Her colleague's list started with a short note and went as follows:

I have known Margot for nearly a year and this list is very different from the one I would have written when I first knew her. To make things clearer I have put in brackets how she would have appeared to me then.

Pleasant (Supercilious)
Efficient
Friendly (Unfriendly)
Perfectionist
Trustworthy
Takes things too much to heart (Unfeeling)
Uneasy with strangers (Brusque)

ANALYSING THE RESULTS

By comparing Margot's own lists with those provided by her sister and her colleague, it was easy to pick out certain points which she had not previously realized. She was delighted to be thought kind, pleasant and trustworthy, and quite moved to discover that her colleague thought her friendly – though dismayed that the original impression she had given was of being the opposite.

Because they either remain silent or simply answer questions when asked (usually speaking in monosyllables if possible), people who are shy or lacking in confidence often come across as unfriendly or supercilious – although they are not usually aware of this. But, of course, because this is how they seem, no one feels able to tell them so – and a vicious circle is created. They seem unfriendly so no one talks to them; no one talks to them so they feel they are not liked. Feeling this, they hesitate to make the first approach in case they are rejected; they then seem even more unfriendly . . . and so on. It is only when they realize what is happening and decide to do something about it that the pattern can be broken. And it takes something like analysis of their Inner and Outer Faces to bring about this realization.

Once Margot had reached the stage of understanding how she came across to other people, as compared with how she really felt inside, she naturally wanted to do something to improve the situation.

She thought she knew the original cause of her insecurity and it dated back to her childhood. Her parents were both professional people with busy careers and it was quite common for Margot to be left in charge of her younger sister and brother during the school holidays. Perfectionists themselves, her mother and father would spend a great deal of time reminding Margot of her responsibilities and explaining exactly what was expected of her while they were not at home. When they arrived home in the evening, they wanted a full report about everything that had occurred during the day and, if there was anything with which they were not pleased, they would tell Margot how disappointed they were in her and that they felt she had let them down. However, on the occasions when all went well – and there were many – they did not praise their daughter but acted as if this was the least they could expect.

Margot had spent her early life desperately trying to gain praise from the two people she most wanted to be pleased with her – her parents. Not wanting to disappoint them, she had become almost paranoid about doing anything wrong and thus, while becoming extremely efficient at anything she undertook, she never felt that she had achieved a sufficiently high standard.

Although naturally it is helpful to understand the background reasons for the current situation – particularly if they still exist – it is not essential to do so for Hypnothink to be effective. Even if someone has no idea at all why their present problem arose, it can be overcome by means of Hypnothink.

CHANGING YOUR INNER FACE

An important point to remember is that it is possible to change your Inner Face at any age. In fact, maturity of vision can be a distinct help.

What you are going to learn to do is similar to hypnosis – although on a non-hypnotic level. You are going to change your Inner Face to the one you desire by using your imagination. You cannot achieve this by will-power. In fact, will-power would actually have a distracting and negative effect.

You came into this world with a mind which could be compared to an empty computer – virtually unprogrammed. Gradually you acquired certain patterns, such as those needed for safety and survival. You learned not to touch something which was red-hot, for example.

In exactly the same way as those instincts were fed into your memory cells, you are going to put specific concepts into your mind. Once this information has been properly programmed, your mind – your own computer – will transmit it to your body as and when it is required.

Success and failure

The world is divided into two basic types of people – successes and failures. This even applies to physical health. Some people are constantly complaining about their health and always rushing to consult their doctors. Others will say, 'I'm never ill from one year to the next.' And they are not. There is never a reason for them to see the doctor.

Some people say, 'It doesn't matter how much I eat, I never gain weight.' And it is true. There are even people who overeat to extremes and yet remain slim. There are also those who say, 'I eat like a bird but I still get fat.' And when you check on these people and their eating habits, that statement turns out to be true.

Positive thinking only works when it is consistent with a positive Inner Face. It cannot work if you have a non-successful Inner Face.

People who are successful have an in-built goal-striving mechanism. Their natural instinct is to reach for a target – and because they do so with confidence, they achieve it.

The future in the present

Hypnothink is an exciting concept because it deals in the future.

We have all been conditioned to think of the future as some sort of nebulous abstract. The future, to most people, can be anything. It can bring disaster or it can bring happiness. With Hypnothink you are going to think of the future in the present – and therefore you will be using the future in the present tense in order to achieve your aims. In a sense you will be exploring the future and using the results of those explorations.

It is so important to realize that we learn to be successful by experiencing success. A person who has done nothing but fail knows nothing about success.

My years of experience in clinical hypnosis bring the knowledge that there is no difference between actual experience and imagined experience.

Imagining success

Some time ago I was consulted by Eric, a man in his early forties who was a successful television director and a man of considerable charm.

Perhaps because he spent a great deal of his time with

the 'young and beautiful', as soon as he entered his forties
Eric's Inner Face changed. He became persuaded that his
sexual prowess was diminishing. Gradually he lost his
capacity for sex. He became impotent.

Using the Hypnothink technique he learned that, before
an encounter with his intended sexual partner, he should
fantasize having successful sex with her. He should go
through the motions in every specific detail in his
mind – devoting to the imagined experience the same
amount of time which would be occupied by him actually
performing the act.

Once again we were applying the principle that once
you score a success you can repeat it. In Eric's case, he
Hypnothought a successful sexual encounter with his
chosen partner. Then, in reality, he merely had to repeat
this earlier (imagined) success.

Eric soon found that he was capable of enjoying a
vigorous sex life once more. He had proved to his own
dramatic satisfaction that an imagined experience can be
equivalent to the actual experience. Eric had altered his
Inner Face quickly and successfully.

The next steps are to work out precisely what you wish
to achieve and then to explore the uses of imagination
and apply them to the process of programming yourself
in order to alter your own Inner Face.

3

Planning is exciting

Now we come to one of the most exciting parts of the whole process – planning. Just think, you are going to decide what you want for the future and then you are going to make it happen. That will put you in the top few per cent of the population. Most people simply exist: they take what life throws at them and try to make the most of it. If only they realized that they have the power to make dramatic and exciting changes in that life.

AIM FOR SUCCESS

Of course, there are certain external limitations upon what you can achieve. You are not going to become President of the United States of America (even supposing you would want to!) if you are not a US citizen. It would be impractical to plan to become an intrepid jungle explorer when you know you have a young family dependent upon the salary you earn. If you are severely physically disabled, you are not suddenly going to be totally fit again. Dreams are wonderful things, but for Hypnothink to be successful you need to set your sights at a level which is feasible.

The trouble is that most people do not know what that level is. The majority of people sell themselves very short perhaps thinking that it is better to aim low and arrive than to aim high and fail. But who says you have to fail? Why not aim high – and get there?

You see this tendency to aim low in many areas of life. I do a considerable amount of work as a business training provider, often running seminars for women returners or for people who have been made redundant. These two categories include many whose self-esteem has taken a hefty knock and who therefore seem to believe they are not capable or even worthy of going after a particularly good job.

The women returners may have been out of the workplace for some years – often while bringing up a family. Some of them left offices as shorthand typists but now find that they need a positive plethora of new skills in order to cope with today's computers, modems and fax machines. Sometimes, rather than setting about learning these new skills, a woman will look for a job which, although possibly boring and mundane, she believes to be well within her capabilities.

Anyone who has been made redundant, or who has found it impossible to find work in the first place, naturally feels insecure and rejected. This person, too, is more likely to settle for a lesser job than they are capable of doing, simply because they feel themselves to be less worthy than others.

But the success you are going to aim for does not have to concern only your working life. You might want to overcome a particular fear or phobia, to improve a relationship, to excel at your favourite sport or to pass your driving test. 'Success' for the aspiring business executive might be a seat on the board of directors, while for the agoraphobic it would be walking to the local shops.

Success and happiness

It is important to enjoy the process of becoming a success. Whether it takes you days, weeks or months to reach your goal, you are doing something wonderful and worthwhile – so remember to stop and enjoy it along the way.

Many people have a back-to-front philosophy. 'If only I were successful,' they say, 'I would be happy.' What they should be doing is reversing this line of thought. Be happy and *then* you will be successful.

Spinoza said: 'Happiness is a virtue, not the reward of virtue.' And in his *Ethics* he added: 'Because we delight we can restrain our lusts.'

Literature abounds with sayings which make this point: *happiness creates health*.

When people are gloomy and depressed their friends might say to them: 'Why don't you look on the bright side?' Unhappiness doesn't solve any problem at all. It merely creates new ones.

Happiness should not be dependent on distant hopes. People who think, 'When I have paid off my overdraft I'll be happy; or 'When I have a girlfriend I'll be happy', or 'When I have my own house I'll be happy', are putting their happiness into the future and making it conditional on something else.

There are also many people who acquire the bad habit of reacting according to an established behaviour pattern when things go wrong. For example, they think, 'I've lost my money so I must be unhappy.' Or, 'I've done something foolish so no one will ever respect me again.' Or, 'This has upset me so I must be angry.' The truth is that you don't *have* to do any of these things. There is no compulsion at all.

Robert Louis Stevenson said: 'Being happy enables you to be free from domination by the outside world.'

Outside opinions

And don't make the mistake of allowing the opinions of others to alter your own assessment of events.

Take the case of a woman whose teenage unmarried daughter has a baby. The woman may think, 'What are people going to say? They are going to look down on us.' But this will not necessarily be the case and she needs to separate fact from opinion. The daughter is young and unmarried – that is a fact. She has a child – that is a fact. But the anxieties the woman has and the conclusions she has come to are pure opinion and speculation. The trouble is that, having come to those conclusions, she is likely to act as though they must be correct and she will adopt the manner and bearing of someone who deserves to be looked down upon.

When it comes to making decisions about what you want for your future, you may decide to listen to the opinions of other people but, in the end, you – and only you – must make the final choices. It is extremely important that, for Hypnothink to work and for you to be happy with the outcome, you should work towards achieving what *you* want and not what someone else wants for you. You may reach your goals either way, but you will never be really satisfied unless those goals were your own.

Now you can see why the work you have done on yourself so far has been so important. You have spent some time thinking about yourself – who you are and what made you that way – in order to be in a position to make the most appropriate and exciting plans for your future. *Your* future and therefore *your* plans.

Procrastination

Roger had set his heart on becoming a professional artist. For as long as he could remember he had been happiest when working with charcoal, ink or paint. And he was good. When he was sixteen he was offered a scholarship at a prestigious art college but, despite his own pleadings and those of his teachers, his father would not allow him to take it up. He felt that painting was all right as a hobby but certainly 'no job for a man' – and certainly not for his son. He insisted that Roger came into the family business.

Poor Roger had no choice but to agree. He would have been unable to go to art school without the backing and blessing of his father and so he did as the older man wanted and joined the family firm. His intention was to work there until he was old enough and had sufficient money behind him to leave and pursue his first love – painting. But as the years went by, Roger found that he had acquired responsibilities. He met and fell in love with Beth; they bought a house and soon there were two small daughters to take care of. How could he throw away a decent income to take his chances in the precarious world of art?

I first met Roger when he was nearly fifty. On the surface he was an eminently successful man. He was Vice-chairman of a flourishing company, with an elegant wife and two delightful daughters, and lived in a beautiful home, drove an expensive car and took his holidays in far-off, sunny places. But below the surface there was something lacking – something which all the trappings of success could not make up for. All his life he had been putting off the one thing he really wanted to do. It was always easy to find a reason – the company was expanding, the children required so much attention, their social life was so demanding. Painting was something he was always going to do some time in the future. But that future never came.

Of course, it is possible that Roger would not have been a successful artist. But at least he would have tried to follow his dream rather than living with an aching void all his life. If it had seemed too precarious a way of earning his living, he could have devoted some of his spare time to studying and practising. He may have earned a little less money – but he might have been a far happier man.

Choose what you want for the future – now!

Now it is time for you to decide precisely what you want to achieve – and be sure that you are precise, for what you imagine and what you use Hypnothink to attain is what you will get. So don't simply tell yourself that you would like to be 'happier' or 'more confident' – those words are far too vague. In just what way would you like your life to proceed so that you were happy with it? How would you like to change so that your new-found confidence was evident?

If you are one of the majority of people who has never actually sat down to work out what they would like their future to be and what success would mean to them, now is the time to start. You will find below a step-by-step plan which should help you.

Along with me and the rest of the world, I am sure you have more than one area of your life you wish to improve. But for Hypnothink to be effective, you need to concentrate on one thing at a time. You might want to be a respected business executive who does not smoke, roller skates to championship level and simply loves spiders – and all this can be achieved, but only by taking it one stage at a time. Hypnothink requires concentration and focusing of the mind, and to try and achieve too much simultaneously would simply be confusing and counter-productive.

If you are ready to begin making plans to change your life for the better, let's look at how to go about it.

Step 1:

This stage requires that you use your intuition, and it should be completed as quickly as possible so that you do not have time to question your first, spontaneous answer.

Read the paragraph below and then say aloud the first thing which comes into your head. Don't stop to wonder whether it is possible or not, whether you are being foolish or what other people would think of you. Just say it!

A good fairy has just come to visit you. She tells you that she is able to grant you one wish. You can choose any improvement in your life for your future – what would it be?

Did you give a spontaneous answer? Good. Remember it – write it down if you like – because *this is what you are going to work on with Hypnothink.*

Step 2:

Because Hypnothink involves use of the imagination and visualization techniques, you need a picture or a series of pictures on which you can focus. So look back at the answer you just gave and create a visual image to go with it. For example, if you want to overcome a fear of flying, you could picture yourself boarding an aeroplane and then sitting back and enjoying the flight. If you wish to excel at your favourite sport, imagine yourself receiving an appropriate medal or award. If you would like to be able to speak in public, the image you create should be of yourself standing on a platform addressing an audience; you should be looking confident and relaxed while your audience appears interested and approving.

Don't worry if, as someone with a fear of flying, you don't like the picture of yourself travelling by air – that dislike will be overcome (and indeed reversed) when you come to practise the Hypnothink technique. You do not have to spend too much time now concentrating on the visual image – all you have to do is decide what it will be.

Step 3:

Hypnothink alone would be effective in helping you achieve your goal, whatever it may be. But this and the following steps will help to back up the technique and make the results even speedier.

Step 3 requires a little more thought than your instinctive response to Step 1. But don't spend too long worrying about your answer; just think for a few moments and then write it down.

Bearing in mind your reply to Step 1, if you are to achieve the success you imagined, what would be a necessary half-way stage?

Using the examples already given, if you want to overcome your fear of flying, perhaps you could make a trip to an airport. There you could watch the planes through the huge plate-glass windows, see them taxi along the runway and take off, and observe them coming in to land. Look around the airport building and be aware of how many people there are, all waiting to embark.

If you have chosen sport as your area of improvement, perhaps you could undertake some special training or extra practice which would help you improve physically.

If your answer to Step 1 was to be able to speak in public, you could join a public-speaking class or a debating society so that you have more opportunity to practise and also to hear others speak.

Step 4:

Now you have to use the logical side of your mind as opposed to the intuitive. Keeping in mind your reply to Step 3, think about the following:

If you are to achieve the half-way stage you thought about in Step 3, what can you do this week to set things in motion?

No matter how busy you are this week – you can find the time to do something which will count as the first stage in your success.

If you have a fear of flying you could:

- Get hold of a book with pictures of aircraft and look through it so that you become accustomed to seeing them on a daily basis.
- Set aside a date – and enter it in your diary – for that trip to the airport.
- Go to the travel agent, pick up some holiday brochures and look at all those places you could visit if you went by air.

If you want to improve your sporting prowess, you could:

- Practise some general fitness exercises so that you will be better prepared for the extra training you have been considering.
- Go and watch an expert in action – amateur or professional – so that you are even clearer in your mind about what you wish to achieve.
- Rent a video depicting your chosen sport being performed really well.

The prospective public speaker could:

- Find out whether there are courses in his/her area for public speaking.
- Read a book which would explain the basic rules of a good talk.
- Go and listen to a speaker, on any subject, and observe what they do and how they do it.

Step 4 is particularly important. Even though the task to be performed might be small and seem a very minor step on your road to success, none the less it is a positive step and one which enables you to tell yourself that you are beginning to take control of your life by working – in however slight a way – towards the future you desire.

time you are using Hypnothink as a deliberate mea.... onvincing your subconscious mind that you are the success you wish to be, it is beneficial to surround yourself with positive thoughts on the subjects. Even if you do not stop to contemplate these thoughts in any great depth, the fact that they are around you all the time will have an effect upon your subconscious mind, and this will reinforce the work you are doing with the Hypnothink technique.

The best way to surround yourself with positive thoughts is to use affirmations. These are positive statements relating to your aims and ambitions, which can be written down or spoken aloud – or preferably a combination of the two.

An affirmation is simply a phrase which assumes that you have already overcome your problem or achieved your goal. It is very important to remember that is not an indication of the fact that you are trying to do so. For example, the affirmation of someone attempting to quit the smoking habit would *not* be: 'I am trying to give up smoking', as this allows for the possibility of failure. The affirmation would be 'I am a non-smoker', which assumes that success has already been achieved.

Using the examples we have been working with so far, the affirmations might be:

- *I am relaxed and happy when flying*. Note that here it would not be right to say, 'I no longer have any fear of flying', because the inclusion of the negative word 'fear' would remind the subconscious mind of its existence. Hence the use of the positive phrase 'relaxed and happy'.
- *I can run faster than ever before.*
- *I enjoy speaking in public and I do it well.*

Once you have chosen the appropriate affirmation for your particular situation, make it a habit to repeat it three times at intervals during the day. You don't have to stop what you are doing to concentrate on the words you use; you may even find yourself using them more as a chant than an actual phrase. Listening to the words consciously is not what we are after; as long as you repeat them regularly, they (and their meaning) will penetrate your subconscious mind without your even being aware of it.

Affirmations can also be written on pieces of paper or card and left around in those places where you spend a lot of time. Perhaps the best method is to use those yellow 'post-it' stickers, which you can position wherever you like – on doors, walls, mirrors, the fridge – but which can quickly be removed should you wish to do so. Here, too, it is not necessary for you to stop and read those notes. Your eyes will see them, your brain will register them and the message will be transmitted to your subconscious mind whatever you do.

Step 6:

Because Hypnothink uses a combination of relaxation, visualization and emotion, it helps if you can recall a moment of achievement in your life which caused you to feel happy, excited, positive or successful. This can later be linked with the visual image.

I'd like you to pause now and think of some moments of success in your life. Before you say that there are none, remember that I am not asking you to come up with something that would necessarily be a success to the person you are now, but something which was a success to the person you were at the time it happened. To a five-year-old child, managing to ride a bicycle without the use of stabilizers – and without falling off – is a great achievement, although to the adult who has been a cyclist for years it is trivial and unimportant. You may be a long-distance swimmer today but do you remember the first time you swam a width? How did you feel? Even the cordon bleu cook had to start somewhere and must have experienced a feeling of elation after baking the first perfect sponge. And I think that all those of us who can drive will remember the wonderful moment when those hateful L-plates could be torn up, never to be needed again. So, before going any further, take the time to remember a moment of success which occurred at any time in your life.

You will have noticed that, for the moment, I am not linking that instance of success with your current aim. I don't want you to imagine what it would be like to be happy when in an aircraft, winning a race or giving that talk in public. Because you have not yet achieved success in this area, there will still be in your mind the possibility of failure and this will detract from the emotion I want you to create.

When you have decided what that successful incident is to be, try and remember just how you *felt* at the time. I expect you were happy, proud and excited all at once. Think about those feelings now and store them away in your mind to be used with the Hypnothink technique we will be looking at in detail in the next chapter.

HYPNOTHINK IN ACTION

In Chapter 1 I told you about Sandra, the young woman who had developed such a phobia about water that she could no longer wash her face and hands or go out in the rain. To let you have a glimpse of Hypnothink in action, I am going to refer back from time to time to Sandra's case so that you can see all the stages she went through as she overcame her problem.

Sandra completed the step-by-step process in the following way:

Step 1:

For her final goal Sandra had to choose between washing her face and hands and going out in the rain as we did not want to confuse the issue by having two different images. (As it happened, by the time she had achieved success with Hypnothink, she was able to do both, but for the sake of the process there had to be a single image.) She decided that, while she could always use creams to cleanse her face and hands, being unable to go out in a shower meant that there were many days when she found it impossible to go to work and the company was beginning to grow tired of her lateness and absenteeism. After all, living in England, it is impossible to go for very long without having to go out in the rain!

Step 2:

This was quite an easy goal to convert to a picture. Sandra chose to see herself in a smart raincoat, carrying a matching umbrella and walking down the road in a heavy shower of rain.

Having selected her image, she did not spend too long thinking about it as, even though she knew it was only in her imagination, it made her feel uncomfortable. She mentally set it aside to be used later in conjunction with the Hypnothink technique.

Step 3:

Now Sandra had to decide upon a half-way stage to her final aim. She chose turning on the taps of the handbasin in the bathroom and letting the water run over her fingers. (Sandra's case was so extreme and had lasted for so long that in the end we had to use this image as her first 'final goal' and work towards it with Hypnothink. Having accomplished this, she was then able to go on to overcome her fear of walking in the rain. However, for most people it would not be necessary to work in stages like that.)

Step 4:

What could Sandra possibly do this week which would be a very first stage in her progress? It was important for Sandra to make this decision for herself rather than be guided by me as I did not want her to feel that she was being put under any pressure. She chose the following possibilities:

- If there was a shower of rain, she could look out of the window and watch people walking about outside.
- She could go up to the bathroom, turn on the taps of the handbasin and just watch the water as it ran down the plughole.
- She could look at a book or watch a video containing images of people swimming in the sea or in a pool.

I asked Sandra which action she would prefer to do, and she chose the second one – turning on the taps in the bathroom. She did this several times during the week and, although she did not feel completely happy with it, she felt she could cope, as the water never actually touched her in any way.

Step 5:

By this time Sandra and I had decided that it would be better to work on simply allowing water from the tap to run over her hands, and it was to this end that Sandra composed her affirmations. She chose three:

- I enjoy the sensation of water on my hands.
- Water feels good.
- I control the water.

When I told Sandra that it was helpful both to say the affirmations aloud and to write them and put them where she could see them frequently, she hesitated. Having suffered with this problem over many years – and, indeed, with it growing worse – her self-esteem was at a very low ebb. She told me that she did not fancy 'speaking to herself' as she had tried this before with no result and therefore had no confidence in any words she uttered.

Of course, what she had done in the past was not the same as speaking affirmations. She had been angry with herself and upset about her condition and had tried to exert will-power in order to 'force' herself to become better. Because such efforts cause you to become even more tense and rigid, there is no way that such a method can work. Hypnothink, in contrast, relies on your being extremely relaxed and coaxing your subconscious mind to accept the new image of yourself. However, since written affirmations can be just as effective as spoken ones, there was no need for Sandra to say hers aloud. In fact, since her belief in herself was so low, this would probably have done more harm than good.

So Sandra chose to write her affirmations. She wrote them over and over again on 'post-it' notes and stuck them all around her house. She also wrote some on white cards which were small enough to fit in a pocket or a handbag and kept these with her all the time. Whenever she had a few moments to spare, she would take them out and look through them, even though she did not spend too much time concentrating on the words themselves.

Step 6:

I asked Sandra to tell me about three remembered successes in her life. Initially she said she could not think of any, but I pressed her further and reminded her that they could be very small things which just happened to be important to her at the time.

Eventually she came up with three situations – but to do so she had to go back quite a long way as, for most of her adult life, she had been so obsessed with her unhappiness over her increasing phobia that nothing had registered in her mind as a success. These were her three memories:

1. *Learning to roller skate.* Sandra had two older brothers whom she adored. As a child she used to follow them around and beg them to teach her to roller skate as they did. When they finally did so, her sense of achievement was coupled with the joy of being able to keep up with her brothers.

2. *Making a sponge cake.* When she was still quite small, Sandra had decided to make a cake for her father's birthday. It was just a simple sponge, but although her mother had kept a watchful eye on her, she had made the whole thing herself – even putting some rather lurid pink icing on the top. She had been so proud when the family had gathered round the table to eat her cake.

3. *Being chosen for the rounders team at school.* Sandra had never been particularly good at sport, although she was always willing to take part. She was not terribly athletic and could not run very fast. However, she proved to have an extremely accurate eye and was therefore a good goal-shooter in netball and bowler in rounders. For this reason she had been picked as a member of the school team in rounders – something she had never expected to happen.

I asked Sandra to spend a few moments each day thinking of these three achievements and concentrating on how she had felt about them at the time they happened. By doing this she would be convincing her subconscious mind of her belief in herself as a success.

In the next chapter we are going to look at the actual techniques of Hypnothink and how you can put your imagination to best use.

4

Use your mind

The uses of imagination are many. But the faculty of the imagination has been much neglected in modern society. Where people once indulged in flights of fancy, now there is television and other forms of mass media. I am not saying that there is anything wrong with television, cinema, video and the like; but with so many pictures being placed before us, we are in danger of losing the ability to create them for ourselves.

Imagination is the essence of Hypnothink and we have to learn to harness our imagination if we are to gain positive and beneficial results. Intense imagination feeds a set of facts into the brain. Then, when a future situation occurs, the personality reacts accordingly.

Isn't it strange that, even at this stage of human development, when we pride ourselves on the extent of our technological knowledge, comparatively little is known about how the brain works? Scientists can tell us all about cell structure but they cannot explain precisely what process initiates concepts or thoughts.

Therein lies the essential difference between a computer and the human brain. A computer cannot initiate a concept. It can only do what it is told to do – although it will do this highly efficiently.

A human brain, however – even the most lowly – is constantly initiating thoughts, many of which may be of a sublime nature.

In Hypnothink we combine the qualities of the brain and the qualities of the computer. Your mind conceives the idea of programming yourself for the future and creates the visual image for doing so, and your brain is the receiver of the factual input.

The quality of imagination varies from person to person according to how often it is used. Poets and writers, for example, tend to have a fertile, active imagination – their output (and often their livelihood) depends upon it. Some people in other, more mundane, occupations allow their imagination to become lazy. Think of it as a muscle which, when it falls into disuse, becomes atrophied. But everyone has at some time used this 'muscle' – this faculty of imagination. Without knowing we were doing so, we have all tinkered with Hypnothink.

Who among you has not pictured an event with extraordinary vividness – only to find it coming true at a later stage?

Imagination is one of the qualities which separate man from animals. Animals work purely on instinct. We have our own set of instincts, of course, but in addition we have been blessed with imagination. You will be able to relate to the principles of Hypnothink because they will activate your memory-cell mechanism.

The trouble is that most of us use our imagination and our brain erratically. We do our jobs, we watch television, we read a book or a magazine – and in many cases we stifle all creative thought. The vast majority of us are not living up to our full potential.

We each have a need for emotional satisfaction. We need to explore new territories of the mind and the imagination – to cross new horizons. We need to live a fuller life. By changing our Inner Face we can achieve these objectives.

By using our imagination as part of the Hypnothink technique we can acquire new habits. The word 'habit' has two meanings. It can refer to our behaviour or to our clothes. Our behaviour fits us and our clothes fit us. If we have bad habits, it is rather like wearing badly fitting clothes. If we develop new habits, it is like putting on new clothes. They may feel a little stiff and uncomfortable at first, but the more those new habits become part of us the better those new 'clothes' will fit.

One of the habits you have to acquire is that of telling yourself that, whatever you are doing, success is a certainty. Say to yourself: 'I will practise every day acting the part of the new person I wish to be. There is absolutely nothing to stop me from being happy. I will not allow myself to be pessimistic.' These are rules of living. Stick to them.

LIVING WITH CHANGE

There are many people who find that they cannot live with themselves when life or circumstances thrust new habits upon them. Many of us envy those who have won large sums of money on the football pools, for instance, and yet they include an inordinate number of people who later attempt suicide at some stage. Yet, ironically, these same people have spent a large part of their lives thinking: 'If only I could win the football pools, everything would be all right and I would be happy.' When they do win, what happens? As often as not their world comes apart and they suffer a crisis of self-identity. They may think that because they have acquired a great deal of money, they will now have to play a role in life quite different from the one they were playing before.

That, of course, is the opposite of the programming process of Hypnothink.

These unfortunate 'winners' try to play the part of someone they are not, rather than programming their Inner Face to create a new person within themselves.

Because they have adopted the role – or the habits – of someone they are not, the habits do not fit but end up causing friction, discomfort and feelings of inferiority and unhappiness. They torment themselves with such thoughts as; 'I can't associate with moneyed people . . . I am not like them and they will not accept me.' They cease to think in terms of what life has in store for them to look forward to and start to think in terms of what is expected of them now. They become aimless; life has lost its purpose and its goal.

Looking forward

Everyone needs something to look forward to. It is a waste of time to look back repeatedly on past errors. You need to look forward with pleasure to the goals you hope to achieve. When there is nothing to aim for, there is nothing to live for.

How many men retire from active work and then die soon afterwards? And how many carry on a highly active work schedule and live well beyond what is considered normal retirement age? Retirement is wonderful if you look upon it as a beginning of the next stage of your life rather than an ending of your useful existence. The goals you head for do not have to be work-related: you might strive to have more time to go fishing, write an opera or swim with dolphins. The choice is yours – the goal is yours – the important thing is that there *is* a goal.

Accepting the truth

It is a trait of human nature that we do not like to admit our mistakes to ourselves. So we misinform ourselves. Yet truth is essential and communication with ourselves is vital.

Huge businesses have been known to fail because a

tyrannical tycoon would not listen to bad news. If a member of staff said that an aspect of the company was doing badly, they would be reprimanded or banished from the 'great one's' presence. A natural result of this was that no one was willing to be the bearer of bad news or criticism. So the centre of this vast operation – the tycoon himself – never received the information which might perhaps have enabled him to rectify faults and even save a whole structure from disaster.

Adolf Hitler was just such a man. Whenever a general brought him bad news, he would be demoted or banished. So naturally no one wanted to be the bearer of bad news – which was one of the reasons for the disarray of the German military machine in the latter stages of the war.

A flow of information is absolutely essential.

Sincerity

Look in the dictionary and you will see that the word 'sincerity' is defined as: 'Clean, pure, being in reality what it is in appearance.' Sincerity in the human personality is derived from a combination of self-understanding and honesty. So assess yourself with honesty – but with sympathetic understanding. Most of us find it easy to be self-critical but do not accord ourselves the same degree of understanding we would show to others.

Taking action

Decisiveness also plays an important part in a successful personality – so don't dither. Decide upon a course of action and follow it right away. Those who delay decisions by procrastinating will only find that they have added the element of time to their original problem. But they have not gained any certainty. The fact that you delay the start of something doesn't mean that the project must succeed. It could still go wrong. Of course, if you happen to have made a wrong decision, your plan could still go awry even if you start it right away. The point is, however, that time itself cannot increase the odds in your favour. It is better to make the occasional mistake through taking action than to live in the nothingness of a state of permanent stalemate.

Gambling

One instinct common to most of humanity is the love to gamble. It is those people who do not ever gamble on themselves or their future who seem to develop gambling fever in casinos or on the racetrack. They have always forced themselves to live a life of caution and security so that their natural instinct for gambling has been suppressed. It is just such people who will one day 'have a flutter' and eventually find themselves addicted.

Why not gamble on yourself and your future? Have enough confidence in yourself to test your abilities to the fullest degree.

Ordinary living

You can always begin by practising self-improvement on minor issues. Ordinary living on a day-to-day basis takes quite some doing. Every day is full of petty challenges and problems. So start by adjusting your programme of self-improvement in ordinary living.

An important fact to bear in mind is that, in order to be a successful personality – and to believe in yourself as one – other people's feelings have to be considered. The more you can make other people feel important and esteemed, the more important *you* will be to *them*.

Self-doubt

Carlyle once said: 'The most fearful unbelief is unbelief in yourself.'

Whenever you hear someone say, 'I just can't do it', you know that person has lost the game of life. While no one appreciates being in the company of a braggard, there is no virtue in being excessively humble and self-denegrating.

Self-doubt lies at the heart of all jealousy. Never dramatize yourself as an object of pity. Don't say, 'I feel sorry for myself', and don't be afraid of appreciating your own virtues. Pride in your own worth only becomes egotism if you assume that you created yourself and should therefore take the credit for that creation.

Self-confidence

Confidence in oneself is built up by the experience of success – whether that success is real or strongly imagined. Therefore, when you are conjuring up your mental image of yourself, be sure that you remember those past successes you thought about in the last chapter – however minor they may be – and concentrate on them. Forget the failures which come to us all from time to time.

Too many people dwell on their failures and constantly remember them. This is the surest way to destroy any remaining vestiges of self-confidence. One remembered success can obliterate the effect of hundreds of failures. So forget the failures and let the successes reinforce each other. At the same time, don't live a lie, pretending to be someone you're not. You are still you, but a more successful – and therefore more confident – you.

The self-image you create for yourself must be compatible with your personality. You cannot change the intrinsic *you* in the sense of transforming yourself into a different person altogether. But you can certainly discover far more about yourself that you can truly admire, and you can rid yourself of those failings which are not so admirable.

Making mistakes

If you make a mistake, that does not mean that you are no good as a person. It simply means that you made a mistake – which you won't necessarily make again. If you make an honest assessment of yourself, you are bound to find imperfections. Learn to tolerate these rather than blame or over-criticize yourself for them. After all, no one is perfect (and wouldn't they be insufferable if they were?).

You are no more rendered worthless because you have made a mistake – even a very big one – than a champion cricketer is made worthless by missing an easy catch. A chef whose soufflé sinks is not banished from the kitchen. It is thoughts and principles such as these which can help to induce the right frame of mind for the process of self-programming.

THE HYPNOTHINK TECHNIQUE

There are several stages to the basic technique itself. Some of these remain constant whatever the problem you are trying to overcome, while others will change from person to person and from result to result. It is extremely important that those constant stages are practised correctly, and many people find it easier to listen to the words rather than to read and remember them. For this reason, as well as telling you about them here, you will find them at the end of this chapter written in the form of a script.

You can use this script in various ways. You could ask a friend to read it to you as you practise the technique. This has the advantage of having another voice telling you what to do but, of course, your friend or family member might not be available at the time you wish to practise – particularly if you select the optimum time of just before sleep at night. So you might find the best method is to read the script aloud and record it on cassette. You can then play it back whenever you want – you could use a personal stereo if you do not want to disturb anyone else.

Having the script on cassette to start with also stops you having to think about what comes next or wondering if you have left something out – which would cause you to become tense. Naturally the time will come when the technique is so familiar that you will no longer need your cassette, but it can be a very useful aid in the beginning.

Now, as to the stages of Hypnothink themselves:

1. *Selection of goal and appropriate image*

If you worked through the last chapter correctly, you have already done this. You have decided upon the outcome you wish and have chosen a suitable visual image to go with it.

2. *Relaxation*

For Hypnothink to work effectively, you have to access the subconscious mind, and to do this it is necessary for you to be as relaxed as possible during the process. Of course, all the words and images used will be heard and absorbed by the conscious mind too, but without reaching the subconscious no changes will take place on a permanent basis. Will-power alone is never enough. You have probably already proved this to yourself – by the time most people come to try techniques such as Hypnothink, they have already attempted to accomplish the same thing in several different ways, and failed. With Hypnothink you can succeed.

There are many ways of achieving relaxation – all of which require practice but most of which will give some benefit from the very first time you try. If you are someone who has practised yoga or meditation, you might already have a technique with which you are familiar and comfortable. If this is so, you may be happiest continuing with this method. However, you will find detailed in the script a method which I have been using for years with those who come to consult me, and which works extremely well for novice and expert alike.

Relaxation is of great benefit in many areas of life – not just the one you are trying to improve by Hypnothink. Of itself it changes nothing. The things happening around you continue to happen. What it does change is your reaction to those things and thereby their effect on your well-being.

Various physical changes happen when you are completely relaxed – all of which are beneficial:

• Your heart and pulse rate become slower and steadier.
• Your blood pressure is reduced.

If you are someone whose life is very stressful (possibly through no fault of your own), these first two points alone would be enough to reduce the likelihood of a stroke or heart attack in the long term. In the short term, headaches, irritability and insomnia are reduced.

• Your muscles relax, reducing the incidence of muscle strain or a build-up of tension – particularly in the head/neck/shoulders area.
• You produce less adrenalin (this is particularly helpful

for those women who suffer from pre-menstrual problems, as an excess of adrenalin can detract from the production of the female hormones and thus increase the likelihood of mental tension and physical discomfort).

You cannot experience the above physical changes without being affected mentally and emotionally. You will find that:

- You are less likely to become irritable or tearful over the build-up of comparatively small matters.
- You are able to think more clearly, either about day-to-day matters or in times of emergency.
- You feel more in control of yourself and of situations around you, and this gives you a sense of increased positivity and self-confidence.
- Relationships with others often seem less tense and are therefore more harmonious.
- You are able to find a sense of peace within yourself – something which is sadly lacking in the lives of most people these days.

And all this before you even get to Hypnothink!

3. Creating your 'special place'

Because, as we have already seen, all our lives have been affected from the very beginning by what has happened to us and by the people who have had influence upon us, it is necessary to find a still, quiet place in the mind which is unsullied and uncontaminated by the negative thoughts which those earlier events and encounters may have created. This is possible by following the specific instructions given in the script.

Although the initial instructions for reaching this special place – I like to think of it as a place of tranquillity at the very centre of your mind – will be the same in each case, the place itself will vary. We are all different, with different likes and dislikes, so it would be impertinent of me to describe what your particular place should look like. Not only would it be impertinent, it would be counter-productive – if you did not feel completely comfortable with the mental surroundings in which you found yourself, this would detract from the efficacy of the visualization which follows.

4. Imagine your happy ending

This is where you visualize the outcome you wish to achieve. Visualization is simply the use of the imagination to form pictures in the mind. With the exception of those who had the misfortune to be born blind, each of us has the ability to see pictures in our mind – although some people may feel that they do not.

If you find it difficult to 'see' things inside your head, don't worry. You have simply become so used to applying logical thought to life that you have temporarily mislaid the ability. But because it was once natural to you, it can be so again – it simply takes a bit of practice.

All babies are visual beings. They have to be, as they are born with no knowledge of language. Everything they learn in the early stages is by means of observation. You had that ability as a baby and you can have it again now as an adult. It is rather like learning to re-use a muscle which has been neglected. You will know that if you have not ridden a bicycle for some time or if you have not been swimming for years, trying to do either can prove difficult – you may find you cannot do it for as long or that it makes you far more tired. But it really takes very little time to get used to it once again. And that is how it will be with visualization. Even if you find it difficult to begin with, do persevere and it will come easily and naturally to you – and in a far shorter time than you might think.

Visualization is an intrinsic part of the Hypnothink process, so should you feel that it has become unfamiliar to you, please take the time to stop and re-acquire the ability before progressing to the rest of the technique. To attempt to overcome a problem before you can visualize will probably result in a very minor achievement – if not in complete failure. This would dishearten you and reduce your self-esteem still further. Do avoid this happening to you by pausing here, if necessary, to improve your ability to visualize.

The steps to improving your visual imagination are as follows (if you find the first one easy, start straight away on the second):

a) Look around the room and select any object you can see clearly. It can be something as simple as a book, a cup or a flower. *Look* at that object. Really *see* it as opposed to mentally telling yourself what it is. If it is a book, notice the colour, the size, and whether there is a picture on the cover. Now close your eyes and try to re-create that object in your imagination.

   If you have become unused to using your imagination, you may find this difficult to begin with – but remember it is not a test. If you are having problems, simply open your eyes and look again. Then repeat the process. Soon you will find that you can imagine any single object around you that you choose.

b) Now work on something with which you are familiar, but which you cannot actually see at the moment – perhaps your own kitchen or garden or a building you pass regularly. Close your eyes and try to imagine what you have chosen. If there is any area of which you are unsure, you may find that you need to go and have a look.

c) Once you are able to achieve (b), you can go on to stretch your 'imagination muscle' still further. Think back now to a place or an event from your childhood – something pleasant or enjoyable. Picture it in as much detail as possible. You may find it easier to begin with a single item and then gradually widen the image –

perhaps starting with your favourite teddy bear, then seeing the bedcover it was sitting on before trying to visualize the entire room.

d) Now let's see how effective that imagination has become. This time I would like you to create something entirely new in your mind. Suppose I were to say to you 'picture a house . . . or a beach scene . . . or a country lane'. Each individual person would imagine a different house, beach scene or lane. What would yours be like, I wonder. Try it now. Select one of the three suggestions and create something in your imagination. Since it is your invention, you might as well choose the type of house you would most like to live in, the beach you would most like to lie on or the lane you would most like to walk down.

Once you can do all the above, your ability to visualize will have returned and you are ready to progress to the next stage of Hypnothink.

5. Link in your feeling of achievement

In the last chapter you looked back at some achievements in your life and how you felt about your success at the time. As part of the Hypnothink process you will be asked to recall the *emotion* of that past success (though not necessarily the achievement itself) while visualizing your future success.

This process helps to dispel the feeling we all have from time to time that we cannot do something, or that because we have failed to achieve something in the past, it is to be out of our reach for ever. It is only when the future achievement is approached in a positive frame of mind that the subconscious works to make it a reality.

Imagine your subconscious mind as a computer – it will always reproduce what is programmed into it. If you insert a picture of the future together with feelings of doubt or negativity, then a negative result is what you will get. But programme a positive image *plus* a positive sensation and you are bound to succeed. And you reinforce the new 'programme' each time you repeat it.

Forget what may have happened in the past. By re-programming your mind in this way you are eliminating the harmful effects of any past failures. It is not unlike recording over an old audio or video cassette – whatever was recorded beneath will be permanently erased. Once your subconscious mind accepts you as the success you intend to be, your self-esteem will soar and you will become that high achiever.

6. *Use those affirmations*

While you are working with Hypnothink to reach your goal, it is essential that you surround yourself with positive thoughts and assurances, and this is where the affirmations you have already composed come into their own. Put them on walls and doors; keep cards in your pocket which you can take out and look at whenever you have a spare moment; repeat them aloud to yourself.

Apart from the contribution these affirmations make to the success of the Hypnothink process, you will find that by surrounding yourself with such positive words, your own natural optimism and self-confidence will increase in all areas of your life.

7. *Project forward emotions*

You have seen how beneficial it can be to incorporate into your technique the emotions which accompany the knowledge that you have already been a success at various times in your life. Now stop for a moment and think how you will feel when you have overcome the particular problem you have chosen to work on. What will it be like when you know that something which used to cause you pain or distress no longer has that effect? And, not only that, but remember you have put an end to it *by your own efforts.* How will you feel? Pretty good, I should think – a sense of achievement combined with the exhilaration and joy that come from knowing that you have won! As part of the technique, you will need to draw upon these feelings as you visualize your success.

And now we come to the script, which you can use in any of the ways suggested. Find a place where you will be warm and comfortable and will not be disturbed. The ideal situation is in bed at night, just before going to sleep.

THE HYPNOTHINK SCRIPT

Make sure that you are lying comfortably, legs uncrossed, hands by your sides and eyes closed.

To relax any muscle, you need first to tense it as much as possible. So begin with your feet – tense them and then let them go limp. Now do the same with your legs and your thighs – tense and relax.

Do just the same to your hands and arms – tense the muscles and relax them. And now to the whole of your body – become as taut as possible and then as relaxed as you can be.

Next we come to the area of greatest tension – the shoulders, neck, jaw and face. Be aware of the tension in those muscles and then be aware of the contrast as you allow them to become limp and relaxed.

Now concentrate on your breathing and on establishing a slow and regular rhythm. As you lie there, count from one to ten in time with your breathing. One . . . two . . . three . . . four . . . five . . . six . . . seven . . . eight . . . nine . . . ten.

I am going to give you a picture to imagine and

as I describe it I would like you to see it, feel it and really allow yourself to become part of it.

Imagine that you are looking at an old wooden cart – the type that would be pulled along by an ox or a donkey. The cart has large, wooden wheels and it is on one of these that I would like you to concentrate.

Really see that wheel. It is huge with long spokes and a solid hub at the centre. As the cart is pulled along you are aware that the wheel is turning but the hub at the centre appears to be staying still.

Focus *all* your attention on that hub. Concentrate on it. As you do so, be aware that it is growing larger and larger and larger while you yourself are growing smaller and smaller and smaller. Finally you become small enough to pass through the hub of the wheel – and this is what you do.

Now you find yourself in a very special room. Unlike most rooms, this one is circular – no sharp angles, no corners. This room is personal to you – no one else has ever been there and no one else will ever go there in the future. You can create the room of your dreams. Do that now.

Put into this room whatever you would most like to see. You may choose whatever colours you find most attractive, the furniture and furnishings can be antique or modern – lavish and luxurious or basic and simple.

There is a window in your room and this, too, can be of any style and design you choose – from stained glass to modern double glazing. From that window you can see the scene you would most like to look out upon.

This room is a haven, a place of perfect tranquillity, the still and perfect place at the very centre of your mind.

Take a few moments now to look around your room, to get to know it, to experience the peace of it, to love it. If there is anything you wish to change, you can do so – just as you can change things around in a room of your home.

Leave a few minutes of silence at this point of the tape to allow for contemplation of your room.

In a moment you are going to visualize whatever it is that you wish to achieve. You are going to see tomorrow as though it is today. Before you do so, however, take some time to remember that you are someone who has already proved themselves to be a success. Remember what success feels like. You are an achiever and you can be a success whenever you wish.

Keeping in mind the joy of success, picture yourself as having already achieved the goal you have chosen.

At this point leave sufficient 'blank' tape for you to visualize your desired aim in great detail. It is better to leave too much space for this than not enough.

You have already decided that you are going to surround yourself with verbal and visual affirmations to reinforce what you have been doing. Think through some of those affirmations now.

Leave time to do so.

You have just done something wonderful. You have programmed your mind for success. You already know what success feels like because of past achievements. You should be feeling proud, excited and joyous now because you are an achiever once again.

PRACTISING THE HYPNOTHINK TECHNIQUE

I would suggest that you practise the Hypnothink technique (with or without a taped script) every night before sleep for a period of three weeks. You will probably begin to notice a difference long before that time, but to really reinforce the suggestion in your subconscious mind it is best to continue for twenty-one days.

After that there are two methods of proceeding:

- If, like Sandra, your problem is so great that you needed to divide it and work on half at a time, you can now go on to work on the next part.
- If you have been able to deal with the whole situation in one go, continue to practise the technique whenever you feel like it (perhaps two or three times a week) until your confidence is complete.

You may well decide that you have been so successful that you cannot wait to go forward and work on another problem area in your life. Can I suggest, however, that to avoid confusion you wait at least a month before doing so.

So now you know the basic Hypnothink technique. As you will discover, it can be used to change and improve your life in a multitude of ways.

5

The thought is father
to the deed

There is a great deal of intuitive wisdom in folkloric expressions, even though they are usually misapplied. The phrase 'The thought is father to the deed' acquires a new connotation when regarded in the context of Hypnothink. But will-power plays no role in Hypnothink. If anything, it has a disruptive effect. For a sportsman or woman to repeat over and over again just before a contest 'I'm going to win' is of little use in itself. But should he or she approach the situation on an organized basis by also feeding specific visualized data into the brain, the possibility of winning becomes a logical reality.

A famous quotation states that: 'If the human mind can *conceive* of something, the human mind can *achieve* it.' You don't need to know how to build a car – or even how it works – in order to drive it. Nor do you need to understand the mechanism of a typewriter in order to type. In the same way, you don't need to know how the human brain works in order to use it to advantage.

When you present your brain with a problem, it automatically scans its memory banks for relevant information to enable it to cope with the situation. It has to recognize the problem before it can respond to it.

An inventor has great difficulty if he has to invent something utterly new. To illustrate this point, it must have been comparatively easy to invent television once radio had already been invented. It was known precisely what was required – radio with pictures!

When you apply Hypnothink there is no need to worry about making mistakes because those mistakes can actually play an important part in the whole process. This will be illustrated further in the next chapter.

CREATING A NEW INNER FACE

Let's go back to Sandra and her phobia about water to see an example of Hypnothink programming in action.

- Sandra wanted to be able to turn on the tap and let the water run over her hands. She decided she would like to do this for five minutes. Her programming, therefore, needed to last for five minutes.
- She had to repeat the programming process each night just before falling asleep.
- She had to be specific. It would not be enough to think, 'The water will run over my fingers.' Sandra had to see every detail in her mind's eye and imagine how it would *feel* to have the water trickling over her fingers and how excited she would be at having overcome what until now had been an insurmountable problem.
- While practising Hypnothink, Sandra was not to take into account the possibility of error. There was no need for her to think about the fact that she might not be able to do what she had imagined – her brain would take care of all eventualities and ensure that she could.
- It was very important for Sandra to remember to work in terms of pictures. The brain retains pictures far more readily than words or abstract ideas. Giving herself a comforting verbal account of what she was doing would not be sufficient. Sandra had to *see* the taps and her hands with the water gushing over them.
- *Remember that will-power does not enter into this process at all. Imagination is the key.*

The number of times this programming has to take place before actual success is realized naturally varies according to the individual and to the type of problem being dealt with. Sandra, in fact, found that after the first occasion she could easily turn on the taps and just watch the water. It took about ten days before she was able to place her hands beneath and allow the water to run over them.

Faith

You don't have to go very far back into the history of medicine to the days when many doctors were armed against the ills which beset mankind with only two basic weapons – a brown medicine and a pink one. The brown medicine was rather sour and was for adults. The pink one was sweetish and was for children.

Patients needed a lot of faith in those days because that was usually what determined whether or not they pulled through. If they believed in the doctor, the medicine tended to work. If not, it did not. Faith heals.

THE RELATIONSHIP BETWEEN MIND AND BODY

Hypnothink represents a breakthrough on a subject which has intrigued, and yet often eluded, scientific thought since the beginning of time – the relationship between mind and body in the complex interaction which makes up the human being.

Programming for success

Two tennis players were matched in France. Player A won by six games to love three times in a row. A few weeks later the players were drawn to play each other once more, this time in Britain. Player B approached the match with a tremendous disadvantage. He had a memory pattern of stupendous defeat after the thrashing inflicted on him in France. The other player, by contrast, had an Inner Face of resounding success to buoy up his confidence and programme him for yet another victory.

By utilizing the principles of Hypnothink, player B programmed himself into an attitude of success, and after a ding-dong match he just managed to beat player A. Normally it would have been a rout – a non-contest. But through the adjustment of Hypnothink, two fine players met on equal terms and the truly better player won.

Success does not have to be real. It can be imagined. The effect is just the same.

Learning and examinations

Hypnothink is just as applicable in a totally different field of activity. A student, for instance, might wish to improve his learning capacity in preparation for a particularly taxing examination. Following the principles of Hypnothink, he will visualize himself at the examination desk, reading the questions and writing out his answers. The questions posed will be within the ambit of his knowledge and he will be able to answer them easily within the time allotted. (Of course the student must have done his revision. There is no miraculous process by which a mind can absorb information it has not studied.)

This process will also eliminate problems associated with the examination procedure such as excessive anxiety. It will eliminate too, the arch-enemy of any student – the negative activity of reading without thinking, without absorbing any of the material scanned by the eye. With the proper use of Hypnothink, the student will find learning an enjoyable and constructive action in which knowledge is retained with more than usual efficiency.

Success is good for you

People with a poor Inner Face might say, 'I have nothing to do – I am bored.' These unfortunate people are not motivated towards a target of any sort. They have started a failure mechanism within themselves – and such a mechanism can be self-perpetuating. It provides a justification for procrastination and for avoiding work. 'Why bother?' they ask themselves. 'Why try?' They have trapped themselves on a treadmill of humdrum existence. If, by some fluke, this type of person should achieve a genuine success in some field, he may find it difficult to live with. His instinctive reaction is one of guilt – as though he has stolen something to which he is not entitled. This syndrome is far more widespread than many people realize.

It is essential, therefore, that you accept that you are entitled to take the credit for your own capabilities. Never feel guilty about succeeding. Real success – a target attained – cannot hurt anyone. It is a creative accomplishment and, as such, can only be of universal benefit.

CURING YOUR EMOTIONAL HURT

Emotional hurt leaves emotional scars in the same way – and just as genuinely – as physical injury leaves the legacy of a physical scar. In order to programme yourself for the future, you will have to seek out and recognize those scars.

When people are hurt emotionally they withdraw into themselves. But what they should do is remove those scars – rather like having cosmetic surgery – so that the Inner Face is restored to an acceptable state. The verbal imagery often used in such cases is indicative of the way these people feel. They say such things as, 'I have gone into my shell', or 'I've built a wall around myself.' Just the other day a woman patient who had been betrayed by a man she trusted told me, 'I'll never put myself into a position again where I could be hurt by another man'.

A shell may keep things out – but it also keeps you in. If you build a wall to keep out one hurtful thing, it will also keep away many other things – a lot of them useful and rewarding.

People with this attitude to life will not trust anyone, even if they feel an inner need to be dependent on others. They are often so afraid of being rejected that they are likely to attack first, causing hurt and confusion in the object of that attack. In this way they drive away the very people to whom they find themselves attracted. It often happens, too, that such people seem deliberately to repel or antagonize those who might be able to give them medical or psychological help. The irony of the situation is that their fear creates the very situation that they feared in the first place – alienation.

Restoring your Inner Face

Emotionally scarred people have an Inner Face of being unwanted and disliked. They see the world as a horrid place. Other people are there for combat, not for co-operation. They have created for themselves a world of frustration and loneliness.

No one likes to be criticized, but hyper-sensitivity to criticism is a sure indication of a poor Inner Face. How often have you heard someone say, 'Be careful what you say in front of *him*.' They have learned from experience that here is a person who is very quick to take offence, to see an insult where none is intended. Such a person is hurt by imagined threats to his ego. An intense exaggeration of this process could result in paranoia – a fixed delusion of danger from real or imagined threats to the ego.

This sort of attitude creates an insecurity which need not exist at all. It is necessary for each of us to have some sort of ego protection – a resilience of spirit which enables us to withstand the blows life sometimes aims at our self-esteem. But when people over-react and develop a thick layer of emotional scar tissue to protect themselves against any future injury, they are also robbing themselves of the pleasure of sensitive feelings, of the refinements of enjoyment which are among the richest blessings of life.

When a physical injury is received, it can leave visible scar tissue because of the tension of the skin healing under pressure. If there is no tension of the skin, there will be no scar. This applies equally to the mind and the emotions.

In a state of emotional relaxation it is impossible to feel tension, anger or fear. It is not possible for a fully relaxed person to suffer an asthma attack or a migraine headache.

Physical states of tension come about when someone responds negatively to a particular situation which has become a source of anxiety.

Healing your emotional scars

In the process of programming yourself for the future, it is necessary for you to cut out those old scars which clog up your emotions and obstruct the way for valuable sensations. How do you perform this magic surgery? For one thing, don't worry about *forgiving* people for hurtful actions against you in the past. Just *forget* them. If you forgive rather than forget, you create a sensation of moral righteousness. This could create an even bigger scar because it can become an aid to memory – like a cancer which feeds on being recalled. You recall your righteousness in having forgiven the offender – so at the same time you remember the offence and it rankles.

Never fall into the trap of forgiving someone and therefore thinking of them as being somehow indebted to you. If you do, you will find that when that debt is cancelled, you are in reality creating a new debt.

Suppose a moneylender lends someone ten pounds and charges one pound in interest, due on repayment in two weeks' time. After two weeks the borrower has not repaid the debt. Perhaps he tendered a cheque and it bounced. So the moneylender draws up a new agreement for a loan – the principal amount of ten pounds, plus the one pound in interest which is owed – plus £1.50 which is the new interest due. The debt has now grown to £12.50. If the borrower still fails to pay, the amount will become greater at a progressively swifter rate.

It will actually do you the world of good emotionally if you are able to cut out the grudge completely, rather like a surgically removed cancer, so that the wound can heal cleanly without leaving any scars.

Unfortunately, human nature is such that it often gives us pleasure to be able to feel superior by means of a sense of justified condemnation of others. It provides an opportunity for mental one-upmanship.

But you need to cancel the debt completely. You won't be doing this in order to be generous, to do a favour or to feel morally superior. You will be healthier and happier without these negative feelings.

Forgiving yourself

In the same way that you forget the transgressions of others against you, you will learn to forgive yourself. Think about the nature of self-guilt. It is a wish to change history and change past actions – both of which are manifestly impossible. So tear up the bounced cheque – it can't be cashed anyway. At the same time, recognize your past errors so that your brain can automatically steer clear of them as it aims for future targets.

The terminology you use when assessing things in relation to yourself can be significant. 'I have failed', for instance, means that you have recognized an error, a shortcoming in yourself. This knowledge can prove most helpful in the future. By contrast, 'I am a failure' means that in your own mind you believe that this same error has changed you as a person.

Suppose someone gets a pain in his leg. We say, 'He has a pain in his leg.' We don't say, 'He is a cripple.'

We all make mistakes. It is an unavoidable aspect of human nature that we should do so. But these mistakes don't make you a failure as a person. Be prepared to be vulnerable to error. Who isn't? Don't over-protect yourself. If you should get hurt, you can overcome it.

The essential awareness for you to retain is that you must keep your sensitivity alive in order to create.

In the world of nature, the hedgehog and the oyster are good examples of creatures which have been made virtually invulnerable in terms of their own environment. But who ever heard of a creative hedgehog? Who wants to be an oyster?

BE YOURSELF

In developing your personality and bringing it to the fore so that the rest of the world can see it – and in doing this successfully – you cannot retain any kind of false front.

What better example of a lovable personality can we find than a baby – any baby? A baby has a personality which is instantly lovable because it has not yet learned emotional deviousness or dishonesty. It has not yet discovered guilt. It has no inhibitions.

An effective personality is an uninhibited one. The very word 'inhibit' means to restrain, to hold back. And if you hold yourself back, you are inhibiting your personality. If you are not being yourself according to your Inner Face, then it is impossible for you to express yourself.

Self–criticism

Your sense of self-criticism should be just sufficient to guide you to your target. It should not be potent enough to deflect you in the opposite direction. All self-criticism should be made in the spirit of 'What I am doing is wrong', not 'It is wrong to do anything.' Self-criticism should be subconscious and automatic.

Excessive self-criticism can exacerbate a phobic condition, as in the case of a stammerer or someone with a worrisome hand tremor. A stammerer is usually afraid of stammering on words which begin with a particular letter – and inevitably those are the words upon which he stammers. If he is able to relax and stop caring about whether he stammers or not, quite often the stammer will disappear.

With regard to the person with a hand tremor, picture four separate tasks – walking along a floating log, threading a needle, pouring a drink and putting a key in a lock. In each case the critical failure only occurs at the exact moment of doing it. If the person is too conscious of it, excessive tension will disrupt the performance of the act.

If that log was not floating in the water but lying on your living room floor – and if no one else was present – you would have no difficulty in negotiating it. It is easy to be steady when you have nothing to prove and do not have to try too hard.

Spontaneity

Excessive care in doing something tends to result in doing it wrongly, or being so afraid of doing it wrongly that you end up not doing it at all. Learn to trust your spontaneity. Let the computer in your brain do the work.

When someone says 'I am self-conscious', what he is really saying is 'I am conscious of other people.' Let your communication with others be spontaneous and uninhibited and your personality will bloom.

If you are introduced to a group of strangers and consciously think that you must try to 'make a good impression', you will automatically begin to monitor your behaviour. The immediate result is that you inhibit your creativity rather than letting it flow uninterruptedly. You should never allow yourself to wonder what other people are thinking of you. On the contrary – just be yourself. Extend your personality so that they can find out what you are really like. Otherwise they will never know.

The judicious use of Hypnothink will enable you to overcome all the stress situations which have been touched on here (and others will be gone into in more detail later).

Picture any situation which is normally troublesome to you. Then indulge in a leisurely daydream involving that situation – and in each case bring yourself through it with flying colours. By this method you will remove the worrying possibility of finding yourself in a situation where you feel you cannot cope. Once you have acquired the inner conviction that, no matter what happens in a given situation, nothing can hurt you, you will have acquired an important attribute. It is known as poise.

READING THE SIGNS OF TROUBLE

The clocks and meters of the human mind are more complex and more sensitive than we suspect. Gauges of the utmost refinement record every change, for better or for worse – but all too often we do not know how to read these omens.

The warning signals of nature are far easier to perceive and interpret in the physical sphere. A fever is a sign that you are running a temperature and the body has been invaded by a hostile organism. Pain is a strong and direct warning that something is amiss.

When it comes to disturbances of our emotional metabolism, the brain has its own set of warning lights which herald trouble. These include feelings of insecurity, worry of an undefined nature, moments of despair, frustration and hopelessness, and fits of bad temper which are often out of proportion to the apparent immediate cause. Many of these signals are cries for help and attention – an adult modification of a childish habit pattern.

A baby, for instance, will rage and scream in a tantrum until mother comes along. The fit of temper has focused attention on the baby and brought solace in the form of mother's ministrations. The infant's brain remembers this emotional triumph – a moment of success – and tries to repeat it in later life. But, of course, truly adult people will have long since shed these basic emotional manoeuvres.

More subtle manifestations, such as an ill-defined general malaise, may be signals to us from our brain that we are off course in some way we know to be beyond our reach. Possibly we are trying to impose a new lifestyle upon ourselves without proper preparation. As a result we generate within ourselves the symptoms of trouble and stress. We have no outlet for this pent-up friction, so our personality mechanism begins to malfunction.

Pessimism

It is astonishing how widespread – and how international – feelings of inadequacy and maladjustment are. In California several hundred students were interviewed by an eminent psychologist. About 95 per cent confessed that they believed themselves to be 'different' in some way. When asked to elaborate, most were unable to give clear explanations but said that they felt 'inadequate' or that 'there is something wrong with me'.

If they think that way, then that is the way they will react to life. Such people experience constant fear and anxiety. These strong emotions block their capacity to live life to the full – their conscious mind is knotted with emotional scar tissue.

It is the vogue in some areas of modern psychology to encourage a gloomy view of life. If it is possible to imbue psychiatry with an overall view of life, at present it often seems to be a thoroughly pessimistic one. Instincts of self-destruction are seen and pointed out at every turn and it is considered the norm to suffer from deeply entrenched feelings of guilt and neurosis.

But so much of this unhappiness and misfortune comes from misuse of the brain. Any machine must have a function. And if it is a good machine it will perform its task perfectly. But even a brand new car must be run in to function properly and an unused motor will seize up with lack of use. The human brain can be regarded as a machine for the purpose of this analogy. And it is the most potent and complex machine ever created. Feed wrong data into the human brain and you will breed and perpetuate error. Correct, positive data, on the other hand, will provide the right answers to emotional questions and generate overall harmony.

In the persistent pursuit of improvement, we must continue to move forward. Inactivity or resigned acceptance is not the equivalent of staying in the same place. It is actually a step backwards because, while you stand still, the world and life continue on their way. Think of the dilemma of the tightrope-walker. If he stays in one position, he will sway and fall. He must keep going to retain his balance. So must you go forward – or fall by the wayside.

Many people create a goal for themselves, strive to reach it and then, when they do, they relax. What they should do is set themselves a new target to aim for. As the saying has it: 'Happiness lies in the pursuit of a desire as much as in the fulfilment of it.'

Loneliness

Loneliness is a specific aspect of maladjustment. Many people who regard themselves as lonely owe their loneliness to themselves, because they do not have sufficient confidence to believe that other people could possibly like them. In many of these cases the cause of this pervading unhappiness has been a parent.

Take, for example, the case of a father who does not have the ability to communicate to his son; he gives the appearance of being taciturn and surly. Because the father does not succeed in getting through to his son, the son assumes that *he* is at fault. To a young child a parent is a form of god, without error or shortcoming. The child's logic goes something like this: 'If I can't talk to my father – who should be closer to me than any person on earth – then how can I talk to anyone? If *he* doesn't like me, how can anyone else like me?'

One of the great ironies in the condition of loneliness is that those who suffer from it may courageously try to smile in a bid to invite friendship. All too often, because of their inhibitions, they strangle that smile so that it seems more a supercilious smirk and makes them appear 'stuck up'. So the attempt to win approval has ended in disaster and has turned into an attitude more likely to antagonize than to attract.

Some lonely people quite like to remain that way. They are afraid that the closeness of friendship will expose them to the searching knowledge of others, with the result that their imagined 'unworthiness' or 'inadequacy' will be discovered. It never occurs to a lonely person to make the intial overtures in a relationship. But if that first bond of friendship can be forged somehow, it will often help them to lose their shyness.

YOU CAN DO IT!

While you are remodelling your Inner Face to suit your new requirements, remember that you must not fear the possibility of making mistakes which you think will shatter your new image. Such a fear could create a pattern of uncertainty in decision making.

Accept the fact that no one can be 100 per cent perfect. If you need to be persuaded of this, just think of the world of sport. In cricket, even the greatest batsman in the world can be bowled out. A crack shot does not always hit the bullseye and even the best of footballers has been known to miss a penalty kick.

People who have built for themselves a strong Inner Face do not mind admitting their mistakes. Thomas Edison said, 'Every wrong attempt I make is another step forward.'

Those with a failure-oriented Inner Face often blame bad luck for their misadventures. They can always find a multitude of scapegoats. If all the energy wasted on these excuses for failure could be harnessed in a constructive way, they would be well on their way to success.

To sum up in order to create a new Inner Face you must be active all the time. Don't rest on your laurels – whether real or imagined. Set yourself positive targets – not the passive kind in which you praise yourself for *not* having done something. Don't place your reliance on others in your efforts to achieve new goals. By tapping the mysterious forces which exist within your psyche and your brain, you will unleash reserves of power beyond your wildest dreams.

In the process of acquiring correct programming, however, there are various attitudes which can mar the procedure. We will look at these next.

A QUESTION OF MORALITY

The question of conventional morality is one which confuses some people. 'When programming oneself', they say, 'to be a "good" person, how does one specify what is right and what is wrong?'

What are morals? And in any case, who are we to judge? Without delving too deeply into the complex subject of ethical morality, what we need to remember for the purposes of programming is that 'right' and 'wrong' can be relative to the particular situation. For example, we are taught that it is morally wrong to strike someone. But it is not morally wrong, for instance, if you strike someone who is in the process of attacking an old lady and in this case your action would probably be applauded by society. Don't be too hidebound in your approach to the matter of morality, therefore. Your own conscience is as accurate a guide as any in such matters.

Do you deserve success?

Another aspect of morality which sometimes occurs among those who are applying Hypnothink for the first time is the question of whether or not they 'deserve' the rewards which the system brings them. These unfortunate people are crippled by an excessively puritanical upbringing. For them, creating success for themselves the Hypnothink way – by programming and the adjustment of their Inner Face – seems too easy. They feel that there is not sufficient effort involved and that, as a result, they cannot deserve the rewards which flow from the procedure. This attitude, of course, is based upon entirely wrong conceptions. There can be nothing wrong or dishonourable about adjusting your personalty for the better. Happiness cannot be culpable.

Fear of life itself

Yet another facet of repressive upbringing is a general timidity which handicaps people in many different walks of life.

A common syndrome among those in show business is stage fright. Before going on stage to entertain their audience, many actors and variety artists are caught in the grip of savage anxiety. In some extreme cases this can render the artist incapable of performing.

Leaving aside the world of entertainment, a host of people leading ordinary lives well away from the limelight have what one could describe as stage fright about living. They have a preconditioned timidity – a fear that if they stick their neck out, someone will chop off their head. For such people it might be worth reversing the conventional advice and suggesting that they 'speak before they think'.

Anxiety

We looked at those who stammer in their speech because they are so worried about the *possibility* of stammering. There are also people who stammer in a symbolic way about the act of living. Those who stammer emotionally – who are hesitant about revealing their emotions and thoughts – will find it is much more effective if they can express themselves directly. If you pause for too long, contemplate too deeply, weigh up all the pros and cons, you inhibit the expression of your personality. This act of inhibition, in itself, creates an adjustment to your Inner Face. What you need to do is simply act by yourself and leave it to your brain – your computer – to make the automatic corrections which will keep you on course.

How often do people look back on some tense moment or some confrontation with another person and say, 'If

only I had thought of it at the time, I would have said . . .'
If you are programmed correctly, you will say the right
things at the right time.

HYPNOTHINK IS FOR EVERYONE

The human personality is an inestimably complicated
mechanism. The problems presented by life are innu-
merable. But to every problem there is a solution – and
Hypnothink encompasses most of them.

In the course of my clinical work I meet patients from
all walks of life. Some are very rich, others are poor. Many
are from somewhere in between. Some are professional
people, others work with their hands, or as clerks, or
are members of the service industries. They represent a
complete cross-section of society.

Great wealth does not protect you from being assailed
by feelings of inadequacy. Being poor does not make you
immune from anxiety. And rich and poor, young and old
alike, can be stricken by a grinding lack of self-confidence.
A large proportion of my patients have problems which
are confidence-oriented.

A wonderfully encouraging and uplifting truth about
applying the principles of Hypnothink is the fact that
it produces obvious results right from the beginning.
Hypnothink 'clicks' with people at once. They have an
instinctive recognition of its truths. There is an emotional
trigger response.

A patient might come in and say, 'I've come to see you
because life is just not worth living; you are my last
resort.' The pressures which have brought this person
to such a low ebb may vary considerably, but the root
causes are almost invariably to be found in the influences
exerted on them by their parents or other authority figures
in the past.

There have even been people in their mid-forties who
have been brought to see me by their parents, just as

though they were still children. And in an important emotional sense they *were* still children because their parents had kept them that way.

Using nervous energy

Many patients suffer from lack of confidence, an inability to adjust to society, a general anxiety state. They are, to use their own terms, 'too highly strung', or 'excessively nervous'. As I always explain to them, the emotion of nervousness can be a source of additional strength.

Before a crisis – and during it – it is normal to experience a sense of nervousness. This emotion releases extra reserves of energy within us in order that we can cope with the crisis. Nervousness is usually thought to mean fear, but it can also mean anger, and it can also be synonymous with an occasion of courage. Therefore it is misguided to think of nervousness as necessarily being a weakness. Regard it as an extra reserve of strength to be used by your brain computer as it sees fit.

Before Judy Garland went on stage she used to work herself up into a state of semi-frenzy, a mood of high intensity – in other words, a condition of intense – but *controlled* – nervousness.

Liza Minelli, Judy Garland's daughter, employs the same calculated technique to induce a mood of semi-ecstasy before she goes on stage. Because of this, she becomes an emotional cauldron and her power and passion spill over to enrich the enjoyment of her audience.

Nervousness is 'high spirits'. You are imbued with an excess of nervous energy just waiting to be used. What you have to learn is to channel that energy to your advantage.

The important thing is to evaluate the crises which crop up in your life, because an *excess* of nervousness can be the cause of tension and anxiety. As this excess has nowhere to go, it builds up the pressure within you.

One way of ensuring that you do not manufacture an excess of nervous energy to cope with a critical situation is to imagine the problem reaching its worst conclusion. This will have the effect of making the problem less bad – because the very worst never seems to happen. Because of your excessively gloomy contemplation, the fact that things are not as bad as you expected should be a cause for happiness.

(Don't, however, confuse this process of evaluation with the technique of programming. What I am suggesting here is no more than a device of oblique thinking which might prove useful to some. If you have any doubts about it, refrain from using it at all.)

We all have a natural tendency to exaggerate our crises. How common a phrase is 'to be scared to death'. But if we allow ourselves to be disproportionately afraid of what are, in effect, minor crises, too many of us may fall victim to the common ailments of modern living and suffer from ulcers, strokes or heart attacks.

HOW TO GAUGE YOUR SUCCESS

Once you have put yourself through the process of self-programming, is there any way to establish the degree of success you have achieved? Unfortunately, there is no foolproof test. It would be nice if you could look through a peephole and scrutinize your Inner Face to see if it had been programmed correctly. A reasonably reliable guide, however, is the state of your emotions immediately afterwards. If you feel good – successful, confident, mildly elated – then you are geared for success. If you are geared for failure, you will feel that, too.

Once you can feel or emotionalize that sensation of success, you can do no wrong. It is a sensation well known to sportsmen and women. They call it the 'winning feeling'. And so it is.

In order to conjure up the taste of success, remember

to call on the memory of minor triumphs. Think back to those successes, no matter how small they might seem to be. Dwell on the sensation. Remember the texture of the emotion. Recall that time when you were inspired to say or do precisely the right thing at just the right moment.

That feeling of success is one which we should do our best to impress on the minds of our children from their earliest days. If a youngster is given a reasonably easy task to perform – one which requires some effort but is clearly within his capabilities – he will immediately experience the success emotion of completing a task with relative ease. Already he will have the basis of the confidence upon which he can build an entire lifetime's attitude. He can be a winner instead of a loser if this initial success is sustained and nurtured with care and sensitivity by his parents.

Think of some of the sayings you know: 'I could feel it in my bones; or 'It was printed on my mind.' Hypnothink has been around – though in an unconscious, uncontrolled and undirected way – for centuries. Now, at last, we are consciously at the controls.

RESEARCH INTO THE EFFECT OF EMOTIONS ON THE BODY

For those who seek rational justification of these claims, there has been a wide range of controlled experiments in various parts of the world which appear to prove conclusively that negative emotions and positive thoughts have a strong – and measurable – effect on the human body.

Tests of emotional telepathy have been carried out by the team of Dr Lutsia Pavlova, electro-physiologist at the University of Leningrad; mathematician Dr Grenady Sergeyev of the A. A. Utomski Laboratory, which was run by the Soviet military authorities; and biologist Dr Edward Naumov. These pioneering researchers found that electro-encephalograph waves changed dramatically when a telepathic recipient was given successive emotions of a negative character. In fact, the Soviet telepath, Nikolaiev, has said, 'There is one kind of test I really hate – the test with negative emotions. That can sometimes make me sick for hours.'

These Russian scientists have proved that negative emotions have a disastrous effect on human physiology as well as psychology. The mind responds in a marked way – and so does the body.

Equally, cheerful and positive thinking helps the body to strengthen and improve its resources. Research carried out in 1956 by Drs S. Serov and A. Troskin of Sverdlovsk, demonstrated that the number of white blood cells rose by 1500 after they had suggested positive emotions to the patients. After the impressing of negative emotions, the white cells decreased by 1600. White blood cells, or leucocytes, are one of the body's main defences against disease.

Dr Pavlova reported: 'Transmission of several successive emotions of a negative character called up the appearance of cross-excitation of the brain. It changed the spontaneous ECG character to the tired state of the brain dominated by slow, hypersynchronized waves of the delta and theta type.'

Dr Pavlova noted that: 'Receivers themselves experienced unpleasant bodily sensations and strong head pains.'

After telepathic transmission of positive emotions, such as calmness and cheerfulness, the ECG became normal once again within one to three minutes; the unpleasant bodily symptoms also disappeared. For further details of this research, refer to *Psychic Discoveries Behind the Iron Curtain*, edited by Sheila Ostrander and Lynn Schroeder, published by Sphere, 1976.

6

Obstacles are there to be overcome

W e are living in a technological age. Man has walked
on the surface of the moon. Missiles can bridge
continents. More and more people are using computers,
and these computers are dealing with increasingly sophis-
ticated tasks. It seems fitting, therefore, that Hypnothink
should make use of a missile-age principle in its applica-
tion to human aspirations – no matter how significant or
subjective they may be.

NEGATIVE FEED-BACK

What happens when a missile is launched at a moving
target? The situation is one of constant flux. As the
missile proceeds towards its target area, it transmits
back to its controlling computer information about its
actual position and its position in relation to the target.
The target, meanwhile, keeps moving. The missile reaches
the point at which it was originally aimed but the target
is no longer there. The missile feeds back the information
that it has missed – and the computer redirects it to the
new position of the target.

In other words, the process is one of continuing error,
subsequently corrected, until finally the missile reaches
its target. That process is known in technological jargon

as 'negative feed-back'. In Hypnothink precisely the same principle will come into play in your brain.

Let's suppose, for example, that you are overweight and have decided to Hypnothink yourself slim. You have changed your Inner Face. You have 'seen' yourself wearing those clothes which will fit you well, flattering your slim outline. You have pictured yourself enjoying only those foods calculated to help you lose weight slowly and consistently until you have reached your target weight. You have imprinted a vivid picture upon your brain.

Then, a few days into your get-slim programme, you are offered a slice of cake by a friend. You pick it up and begin to eat. Three-quarters of the way through you remember with a start that you should not be eating it at all. Your programmed brain receives the negative feed-back: 'This is *not* the right thing to eat in terms of the goal I have chosen', and you find that you do not fancy any more of it. After that you will refrain from eating cake again (you may even develop an instinctive dislike for it) until your target has been achieved and your weight has been stabilized at the desired level.

The point to remember is that, once you have programmed yourself, you no longer have to make a conscious effort not to eat certain types of food. Your 'computer' just won't allow you to eat the wrong things. Each and every time you move into the path of error, an alarm bell will ring in your brain. The effect of this is to nudge you back on course again until you finally reach your target.

A good analogy is that of an aircraft landing in thick fog. The pilot cannot see a thing so it is no use him relying on his own vision. He has to make use of radar. If that pilot proceeds to make a perfect landing the radar will give him no indication of this. But as soon as he veers off course, the radar system will alert him to this fact and he will be able to make the necessary correction to ensure an accurate landing.

Whoever invented the practice swing in golf was,

in fact, putting into practice this theory of negative feed-back. Nearly all golfers take a practice swing before they take an actual swing at the ball. With many of them it may not make the slightest difference – they may play a bad shot anyway. But top-class golfers have been using a technique not unlike Hypnothink for years – as have the top players in many other sports. The champion golfer does more than simply take a practice swing. He strongly imagines that he is hitting the ball, connecting with the correct velocity and precisely the right torque. He will 'see' the ball hurtling through the air and watch it land on the green. As he takes his practice swing, all these events take place brightly and clearly in his mind's eye. It is only then that he steps up to the ball and takes a swing with his club. At that moment his memory cells, programmed by his own vivid prevision, create precisely the muscular effort which is required to match his mental conception of the event. He duplicates, in effect, what he has previously conceived in his imagination.

I taught this same process to a young golfer a couple of years ago and, from that moment on, his game improved dramatically. Of course, he naturally kept up the procedure of having a practice 'think' before actually playing the ball. His friends, observing his actions and seeing the improvement in the quality of his golf – but having no idea of what was going on in his mind – put it all down to that practice swing. So they began to emulate him, but could not understand why their practice swings did not have the same improving effect on their own game.

We all use negative feed-back all the time, but on most occasions our brain does it instinctively so that we do not necessarily realize what we are doing.

Think of what happens in a cricket match. A batsman hits the ball and it flies to the boundary. A fielder decides to intercept it. He runs to catch it. This apparently simple action means that his brain has to work out where the ball will fall, the speed at which it is travelling, the subsequent decrease in velocity, the probable increase or decrease in his running speed in order to meet the ball at precisely the right moment, and how to control the mechanism of his hands so that the fingers close at exactly the right second to pluck the speeding ball from its flight path.

That is missile technology – negative feed-back. But, of course, the fielder doesn't consciously think about all those things – he simply does them. His brain sends the appropriate messages to the muscles which propel his body in exactly the same way as the computer sends instructions to one of the missiles under its control.

Many people – particularly those in the world of sport – have a hazy sort of awareness of this process and of the efficacy of Hypnothink within their own lives. Sometimes these people will convert this semi-subliminal awareness into superstition or ritual. A tennis player, for example, may be concerned with throwing the ball a certain height into the air before serving, in the belief that if he doesn't do this he will be unlucky. What he is really doing is reproducing an occasion when he threw the ball in just such a manner and produced the best service of his life. His brain is attempting to reproduce the experience of success.

It is important to remember that you must not try consciously to make this process work. Your brain will function quite automatically. For example, if we move suddenly into a cold temperature, our body informs us of this automatically. It tells us when we are hot or when we are frightened. The human brain has 'clocks' and 'meters' which science does not yet begin to understand.

In order to dramatize the principles of Hypnothink I have drawn comparisons with computers and missiles. But other pieces of equipment are given negative indicators on a visual level. Think of the common household iron, for instance. It can come equipped with a red light to indicate when it is overheating. In using this sort of equipment, the user is aware of the negative indicators, but not to an overriding extent. This awareness does not actually hinder us in the task we have set our mind to – ironing the sheets, for example.

The same attitude should apply in the use of the Hypnothink process. We must be able to 'glance' at our negative indications without becoming obsessed by them as this would have a counter-productive effect.

If a golfer knows that there is a sand-trap in his path, it is enough for him to have that knowledge. If he *concentrates* excessively on that trap, he is quite likely to put the ball right into it. His target is the green – that is what he should concentrate on while remaining *aware* of the existence of hazards.

When we programme ourselves for success, we substitute positives for negatives. We let our brain guide us out of danger. If you have programmed yourself well, your brain will steer you away from trouble and on to the path of success with the aid of automatic reflex and negative feed-back.

PERSEVERE!

It is all too easy, when you have been suffering from some long-term problem, to try for a while and then find the effort too great and give up. With Hypnothink the results tend to become apparent relatively quickly so this tendency is reduced. However, there are some points to bear in mind:

- *Progress is not always smooth and even.* There may be occasions when you seem to take giant leaps forward, while at other times it is all you can do to take one small step. Don't let this worry you. Your subconscious is working all the time to help you achieve your desired result.

    Emma was an agoraphobic with whom I worked some time ago. When I first met her, she was unable to go anywhere alone – even to the post box at the end of the road. Because her problem was so great, we decided to work in stages. First she had to be able to stand by her open door and look out; then to take a few steps down the garden path; then go through the gate and along the road to the first lamp-post, and so on. Some of these stages were accomplished almost overnight while others took as long as ten to fourteen days. But she got there in the end and completely overcame her agoraphobia.

So, not only should you not worry if your progress sometimes seems erratic, but you should tell yourself that the very worst that can happen is that it will take a week or two longer than you had hoped to be rid of the problem for ever. If this is something you have been living with for a prolonged period of time, what difference does an extra couple of weeks make?

- *Be sure that you have set yourself achievable targets.* Particularly if the problem is a long-standing one, such as a lifelong phobia, it may be necessary to break it down into smaller chunks which can be more easily accepted by your logical, conscious mind. Have no fear, your subconscious can cope with making that giant leap, but if you are going to let doubt get in the way because initially it appears that you are aiming for the impossible, just make things easier for yourself by dealing with it one step at a time.

Remember that each step you take is important, and each is an achievement in itself. Not only that, but for the sake of your blossoming self-confidence, the journey is almost as significant as arriving at the destination.

OVERCOMING PHOBIAS

Let's look once again at Sandra and the way in which she overcame her water phobia. Now *I* knew that it would have been quite possible for Sandra's subconscious mind to cope with the image of her walking in the rain and that she would be able to do so quite quickly. But although Sandra obviously wanted to believe this too, she had lived with her ever-increasing phobia for so long that it was too much for her conscious mind to accept that she would really be able to walk in the rain so soon. For this reason, as you will recall, we decided that the first situation to aim for would be Sandra allowing the tap water to run over her hands. You will also recall that her first step towards achieving this was going to the bathroom, turning on the tap and just watching the water run into the basin and away down the plughole. To anyone not suffering from such a phobia this would be a simple and undramatic thing to do. But is was extremely important for Sandra to realize that – in her particular situation – just turning on those taps and watching the water was a great success. It was something she had not been able to do previously and it was essential for her to take the time to be proud of that achievement and to understand that it was an indication that she would be able to cope with all the other stages of her psychological journey.

The image we have of ourselves and our abilities – and which has been formed and reinforced many times over since we were very young – is sometimes so strong that it almost seems to try and inhibit our progress. I will sometimes find a patient who has been happily Hypnothinking their way to success for days when suddenly a negative aspect creeps into the visualization which he or she is unable to shift.

Let me give you an example. Roseanne had been an agoraphobic for years, but not quite as bad as Emma in the earlier story. She was able to go out in the car with her husband and could even walk to the local shops alone – although she did not enjoy doing so and was always pleased to get home again. She had lived her life this way for a long time and, indeed, most people knew nothing about her condition. They simply thought that she was one of those women who 'liked to keep herself to herself'. And so they left her alone.

Because of this, Roseanne had never really made any friends in the area where she lived. Her family became everything to her. She had a husband she adored and two adult daughters who were now married themselves. Her younger daughter had a four-year old son and Roseanne was, of course, the doting grandmother. When Shelley was due to go into hospital for the birth of her second child, it was natural for her mother to offer to go and stay in her house to look after the little boy during the day. Roseanne was completely familiar with the house and was quite comfortable there. Her husband would take her to the supermarket when necessary and there was a small shop just over the road should she need anything in a hurry. So here, too, she would be able to disguise her agoraphobia. But she had one worry. She knew that Shelley liked to take the child to the park in the afternoons and, anxious to maintain the little boy's routine, Roseanne planned to do the same. But how would she – with her great fear of open spaces – ever be able to walk in the park with a four-year old child.

It was this problem that first brought Roseanne to me. Had it not arisen, she would probably have managed to continue as before – even if somewhat miserably. But she could not bear to think that she would let down her little grandson.

All went well in the beginning. Roseanne was able to relax, and as she had a good visual imagination she was able to use Hypnothink to picture herself taking her grandchild to the park. She 'saw' herself walking along in the sunshine while the child skipped and ran around her.

Then one day negativity struck. Roseanne came to me in a very distressed state. She told me that during one of her Hypnothink visualizations, she had been happily walking in the park when she pictured the little boy falling over, grazing his knee and crying to be taken home. Since that first occasion, she had never been able to complete her Hypnothink without that negative image coming into her mind.

What had happened, of course, was that Roseanne's Inner Face was so used to being one which could not cope with being out of doors in an open space that it was working hard to maintain its position and to resist change of any sort.

When this happens the worst thing you can do is try and *force* the negative image from your mind. If you do this, you will immediately become tense (and relaxation is an essential part of the Hypnothink process), plus you will be admitting to your subconscious that a battleground exists. Better by far to make use of the negative image and overcome it in your mind just as you would in reality.

What Roseanne did was to allow the little boy to fall over in her imagination – after all, it is something small children do all the time. Then she let the Hypnothink continue, visualizing herself doing just what she would do if the same thing happened in reality. In her mind she saw herself picking up her little grandson and giving him a cuddle. She imagined herself wiping his tears and kissing his knee better and then seeing another small boy coming towards them with his mother. This turned out to be one of her grandson's little friends from playgroup and – once again, as it would be in reality – the child soon forgot his injury and ran off to play with his friend, leaving the two women to chat as they walked along, keeping an eye on them.

This is how you should deal with any negativity which might arise when you are practising Hypnothink. Whatever happens, don't get angry with yourself or your imagination; don't think you have destroyed all the good work you have been doing – and don't think that you are destined to fail in achieving your goal.

MAKING ADJUSTMENTS TO YOUR PROGRAMME

I have had patients come to me thinking that all was lost. Perhaps the dieter had eaten a piece of chocolate cake or the smoker had had two cigarettes since last week. When such things happen, many people immediately see themselves as failures and think that the technique is not going to work. And yet – provided they return to the re-programming of their Inner Face – what is the worst that can happen? Maybe the dieter will take an extra week to reach target weight, which is not such a terrible thing, particularly as we are talking about the final week – and most people cannot tell if someone still has a couple of pounds to lose. The smoker was presumably getting through several cigarettes a day or it would not have been considered a problem in the first place. And yet, instead of praising himself for having given up so many, he is thinking only of the two he had. If someone had told him just a few weeks earlier that he would soon be smoking two cigarettes a *week* rather than, say, twenty each *day*, he would have been absolutely delighted.

So remember to stop and appreciate the successes along the way and build any negative mental 'hiccups' into your visualization, allowing yourself to come up with a reasonable way of overcoming them. You will still achieve your goal – even though it may mean taking a slightly different approach.

· If you were about to set off in your car to travel to the coast for a holiday and, while following your usual route, you came across a set of roadworks and a 'Diversion' sign, what would you do? I doubt very much that you would decide that it was not going to be possible to reach your destination and that you would have to cancel the holiday and return home. No, you would follow the diversion signs and make the necessary detour until you were able to return to the road with which you were familiar.

Hypnothink requires just the same of you. Whatever errors you may make or difficulties you may encounter along the way, you will not be prevented from overcoming your long-standing problem or attaining your new goal.

There is no getting away from it – your Inner Face is just going to have to get used to the fact that you are going to succeed!

7

Let the doorbell ring

In an increasingly complex world, tensions are imposed upon us in a million subtle ways. That is why there is still such a huge market in tranquillizers – pills designed to render you indifferent, in one way or another, to the stresses and strains of the world. But we can take a mental tranquillizer rather than a physical one. There are methods of thought – devices of the brain – which can be used to neutralize the destructive onslaught of tension.

COPING WITH STRESS

The purpose of a tranquillizing pill is to make us less aware of outside aggravations and to diminish our anxiety quotient. But one simple way of tranquillizing ourselves is to *ignore* these stresses and strains – to fail to respond in any way to an outside influence.

Conditioning

As we progress from infancy through youth to adulthood we become conditioned to a huge variety of outside stimuli, differing enormously according to our individual upbringing. But for all of us there exist danger signals which induce in us a state of mind stemming from our early experiences. We have unwittingly been programmed by life. Now that we have discovered Hypnothink, we are able to reprogramme ourselves in a more desirable way.

Many of us do what we have always done without stopping to question just why we do it. And often the reason is nothing more than the fact that we grew up around someone who acted in a particular way. Take the child whose mother was terrified of thunderstorms and always rushed to shut the windows and draw the curtains before sitting rigidly in a corner of the sofa until the whole thing was over. That child is quite likely to grow up just as terrified of thunderstorms as her mother without ever pausing to ask herself exactly what she was frightened of. We all know that it is sensible not to shelter under trees when there is lightning about and, of course, occasionally a house is damaged in a storm. But such incidents are rare and for the most part the storms we encounter consist of nothing more than a lot of rumbling and the occasional streak of lightning. So why the terror?

Fears – and indeed reactions of all sorts – may be learned without a word ever being spoken. The hypothetical child just mentioned was not so much frightened of thunderstorms as of her mother's fear of them – a fear that was absorbed rather than rationalized. In the child's mind, mothers and fathers are strong, all-knowing people and it is extremely distressing to see one of these giants go to pieces. Not only does it shake one of the constants of the child's world but it impresses on her mind that whatever it was that caused this collapse must be terrible indeed. In such ways, otherwise kind and caring parents can unwittingly instill a lifelong fear in their children.

Nick was a normal, happy, healthy little boy, loved by his parents. When he was three years old, the family decided to take a summer holiday on the south coast – some two hundred miles from their home. Not really understanding what a 'holiday' was, Nick none the less was caught up in the general anticipatory excitement: 'You can't wear that, I've washed it to take on holiday'; 'Do you want to take teddy on holiday?; 'Only three more days until our holiday.' Such phrases, coupled with general tension at home and the sight of open suitcases waiting to be filled, are bound to excite a small child, even if he does not really understand what is going on.

Nick's father tried to explain the concept of a holiday to him. He was told that they would be staying in a hotel, that they would go on something called a 'beach' where he would be able to play on the sand with a bucket and spade, that they would be able to splash about in the sea. He also told the little boy that they would be going on a long journey in the car to get to this magical place.

With all this new information to absorb plus the activity at home, it wasn't really surprising that Nick grew excited and, for the last couple of nights, found it difficult to get to sleep. He even suffered a minor tummy upset.

When the time came to set out, being anxious that Nick would be able to travel well and happily, his mother kept asking him if he felt all right and told him that if he felt the least bit sick he should tell her. Until that moment it hadn't occurred to Nick that he might feel sick – after all, he had never had any problems in the car before. But perhaps there was something different about holidays.

The matter wasn't helped when his mother turned round every few moments to ask him if he still felt all right. Of course he didn't. Everything combined to make him feel – and then be – physically sick.

From that time onwards, throughout his childhood, Nick was regularly car-sick when going on holiday or any other long journey. The significant thing was that he would be car-sick within ten minutes of setting out – and yet he was able to travel in the car to visit his grandparents who lived some twenty minutes away without any problem at all.

So you see how being programmed from early child-hood can cause us to react spontaneously to stimuli which might otherwise never have bothered us.

There are people who will say that at work they are confident and happy 'until I have to talk to the boss – then I just dry up'. Others may be affected by strangers, by enclosed spaces, by open spaces, by heights, by insects ... the potential list is a very long one, limited only by the human imagination. For one reason or another these people were led to believe, earlier on in their lives, that those particular objects or situations were dangerous, menacing and anxiety-inducing.

OVERCOMING NEGATIVE CONDITIONING

This chapter will explain how you can short-circuit these responses and eliminate them altogether.

A good example of a conditioned response is what happens when someone rings your front doorbell. You get up and answer it. But suppose you are very tired and alone. You may decide to ignore the bell and remain in your chair, relaxed and hoping whoever it is will go away.

You can do exactly the same in your mind. Relax! Let the doorbell ring! Ignore it. You don't *have* to take notice of a danger signal. After all, it is only a signal – not a compulsion. And the danger is not a valid one anyway.

Reprogramming your Inner Face

Evaluate yourself to find out what your personal danger signals are. Then programme your Inner Face to ignore the signal. Your new Inner Face will ignore these signals from now on.

If you are a person who has been afraid of heights, for example, and every time you climbed a certain number of stairs you received a danger signal, you will find that this no longer happens. You are letting the doorbell ring – you are happily climbing the stairs.

Delaying your response

Another method by which you can neutralize these danger signals is to delay your customary response. In *Gone with the Wind* Scarlett O'Hara used to say: 'I won't think about that today, I'll think about it tomorrow.' This can be a very useful technique – provided you never carry it to the extreme of never doing anything about anything! But it is a highly advantageous way of postponing an unsettling response.

If you happen to find yourself placed in a position where your mind is startled by some stimulus which you know will create a danger signal for you, try following the old advice and count to ten before you do anything. By delaying your response you have time to clear your mind. This means that you won't have to follow the emotional, conditioned path of response to which you are accustomed.

Relaxing your brain

As soon as you introduce relaxation to the brain, you remove stress. And if you ignore the stress stimulus, that is the equivalent of the removal of stress. In this instance we could say that a lack of response equals relaxation.

When you are about to undertake some physical task you flex your muscles. When you are about to undertake a mental task you flex your brain. If you decide to ignore the physical task, however, you don't bother to flex your muscles. In exactly the same way, you should not bother to flex your brain at the first sign of a warning stimulus. *Let the doorbell ring!*

Escaping to your special place

Multitudes of people, when confronted by the stresses of our modern life with all its assaults upon our peace of mind and its erosion of our tranquillity, think how blissful it would be to get away from it all. Psychologists call this the 'desert island syndrome' and it is recognized as one of the symptoms of the strain of present-day existence.

Well, there is a way by which you can 'get away from it all'. And the wonderful thing is – you don't have to go anywhere to do it!

By using the Hypnothink technique of visualizing that huge wheel and passing through the centre, you can not only enter your own special room but you can pass from that room into a special place – a secret hideaway – in your mind. That hideaway can take any form you wish. You might like to imagine yourself on a sunlit beach, lying on soft, warm, white sand and listening to the gentle lapping of waves on the shore. Perhaps you would prefer to be wandering in the garden of a country cottage, watching the bees and butterflies as they alight on the lupins and foxgloves. Your special place could be a quiet river bank where you are sitting, your back against the warm trunk of a friendly willow tree, just watching the water glistening and gleaming in the summer sun.

There are no limits to your imagination so you can create what is for you the perfect place. And you can go there whenever you wish – whenever you need to escape temporarily from the chaos of the world and recharge your batteries. This is an utterly private place of retreat. No one but you has ever set foot there and no one ever will. It exists purely within your own imagination. It is an avenue of escape from the outside world.

If you happen to be going through a particularly stressful period in your life, try to enter your special place every day and spend some time there.

This concept of a haven at the absolute centre of a wheel combines the human need to belong yet remain apart. Within the constantly turning wheel you have not left life at all – merely withdrawn from it to a state of total tranquillity for as long as you wish. You can find peace without being left out of the forward momentum of life.

Frustrations and tensions will often build up within an individual to such an extent that they have to blow off steam – just like a pressure cooker. Fill a pressure cooker with water, put it on a stove, adjust the stop-cock on top and eventually the cooker will build up so much pressure that it will explode. But if you remove the little stopper, the steam escapes with extraordinary force.

The human mind is very similar. If you build up a head of steam, you must have an escape valve – otherwise there will be the equivalent of an explosion. Many people let off steam by losing their tempers, by shouting, throwing things or showing aggression in other ways. Now that you have your own special place, you can go to it and figuratively scream your head off if you so wish. It is your private place – your own little world. In this way you can release your build-up of tension without hurting either yourself or anyone else.

The probability is, however, that with the knowledge that all is serene and beautiful in your special place, you will not feel the need to scream – even figuratively. It is likely that it will be sufficient simply to be there, to let the peace and beauty of an environment *you* have chosen wash over you, ridding your mind and body of all accumulated tension.

The presence of too much 'steam' is the cause of so much of the insomnia that we hear about today. Countless thousands of insomniacs spend night after restless night in search of sleep but are unable to halt the ceaseless activity of their brains. If this applies to you, then before you go to bed, go through the wheel and find your special place. There you can let off steam and find peace in whatever manner you find most satisfying and appropriate to your particular frustration. Having done so, you will be able to get into bed with an attitude of relaxed contentment – and you will sleep.

This method of creating a highly personal place to go to and withdrawing into it whenever necessary is not unlike some of the techniques of transcendental meditation. It is far easier for newcomers to such ideas to achieve, however, in that it is a more tangible concept. You can actually *see* your place in your mind. You know that you can go to a spot where everything is pleasant and harmonious and you can be at peace with the world.

Motorists are constant victims of the tensions of urban life. The driver of a car, bus or lorry suffers many aggravations – in addition to those tensions with which he is already burdened – when he leaves home in the morning or drives back from work in the evening. All too often these pressures manifest themselves in a dangerous and aggressive pattern of driving or, if the motorist happens to be too responsible a person to allow his driving to be affected, he may vent his spleen on his colleagues, his staff or his family.

Before you even get into your car, retire to your own special place for just a few moments. Savour the peace and tranquillity of it. Put your mind into neutral. When you come back from it and get into your car you will feel – and therefore react – like a different person.

The overwhelming advantage of this technique, of course, is that you can resort to it at any time of the day or night, no matter where you happen to be – whether you are stuck in a crowded lift, trapped on the underground, at home or at work, or jammed in a motionless line of stalled cars (though obviously not while actually driving along). It only takes an instant and – seemingly magically – you can be whisked away into a private place of beauty where peace reigns supreme.

Don't confuse this procedure with the Hypnothink techniques you use to overcome a specific problem. In this case there need be no link between the time spent in your special place and actual elapsed time. You can go there for five seconds or five minutes. It depends entirely on your own whim. With practice you will learn how to transport yourself to that place in the centre of your mind in an instant.

It is not unusual for people to acquire a misleading perspective and to lose sight of the fact that it is the outside world that is affecting them. Rather, they think only in terms of what occurs within their own personalities. But, in fact, it is usually some other person who impinges on their sense of well-being or some external situation which brings about an abrasive circumstance. Now you are able to alleviate the effect of these disruptive external influences by escaping to your secret hideaway – your own special place.

Calm and harmony

The type of reaction evoked by strain depends greatly on how the person concerned has been conditioned in earlier life. As happens in all life situations, we are all in the process of being unwittingly programmed throughout our childhood and our youthful years. In applying the principles of Hypnothink, we must adjust our Inner Face and programme our 'new face' in conditions of calm and harmony.

An old-fashioned – and somewhat barbaric – method of teaching children to swim was to throw them headlong into the water, thus presenting them with simple alternatives – swim or sink! As a result the children swam in order to survive. Survive they did, but they had no swimming technique as such. Even if you were to ignore the harmful psychological effect of such treatment, they will have acquired the most primitive and energy-wasting system of staying afloat. This is not the way with Hypnothink.

Suppose George Smith has to make a speech – and public speaking is often a high-pressure situation. Using Hypnothink, he will programme himself calmly and thoroughly with no anticipation of a crisis disrupting the planned procedure. Having completed the programming, however, if a crisis does occur, his brain-computer will adjust and shift accordingly, without undue strain. The crisis will be accommodated and overcome. Because George is in a state of control and equilibrium, he will be in the best possible state of mind to deal with an unexpected departure from the norm.

Humans can draw many constructive examples from the study of the humble ant. For one thing, the ant has something to show us in its pattern of behaviour during a crisis. In an ants' nest the bustle and activity never cease. Yet, if you were to stand on an antheap and damage its exterior, the ants do not react to this crisis with confusion or uncontrolled behaviour. Immediately all the ants in the vicinity rush to the damaged area and proceed to rebuild it. They do it quickly – but they do it efficiently and methodically.

We can even learn from the behaviour of rats. In an American university rats were kept in a complex maze. Food was placed at various points in the maze. The supply was plentiful and the rats took their time over wandering around in search of the constantly changing food sites. Then some starving rats were placed in the maze. Contrary to what one might expect, the starving rats took four times as long as the well-fed rats to find the food. *Crisis did not help them towards greater functional efficiency.*

The lesson to be drawn from these observations is that, whatever your target, whether it be to deliver a speech, play sport or simply to mix easily with people at a party, practise doing it in a calm and pressure-free atmosphere – and in fine detail.

A basic truth of Hypnothink is that your brain-computer is the greatest ad-libber in the world.

Consider the analogy of a golfer practising his putting on the living-room carpet. He places the ball on the carpet and putts it into a tumbler. There are no pressures upon him. No money is at stake. There is no intensely inquisitive crowd pressing forward behind him. There are no prizes to be won. This is the ideal setting for him to practise in – to programme himself as closely as possible to perfection. Then, when he faces the reality of competitive pressure, he will have the strength of calm preparation behind him and his inner computer will be able to adjust accordingly.

A cardinal rule of Hypnothink, therefore, is that you should always rehearse under non-pressure conditions. Don't expect crises, don't even consider the possibility that they might arise. If you tell your brain clearly and concisely, exactly what it is that you want to happen, your brain will ad-lib and create a way for it to happen, whatever the circumstances which prevail at the time.

THINKING POSITIVELY

One way of achieving 'self-tranquillization' is to refuse to respond to outside influences. But there is another aspect to this. It is possible for you to *invoke* those outside influences as a positive aid in your programming. For example, if you are overweight and are in the process of programming yourself to become slim, picture yourself sitting in a restaurant, enjoying your permitted meal – and watching all those other people around you who are overeating or eating the wrong things. They are making themselves gross and unhealthy while you remain poised and slim. *You* are not doing what all the rest are doing. It is positive abstinence.

The sportsman or woman should always Hypnothink aggressively to achieve positive results. A footballer, for example, should never think merely in terms of a draw –

of not losing. He must not even think simply of winning – but of *trouncing* the other team. This positive approach is implicit in the principles of Hypnothink.

Some people may find at first that, although they have programmed themselves well, they fail to perform as satisfactorily as they would have hoped in their target situations. *Please* do not give up at this point should this happen to you. Persevere. Carry on with the same method of thought. The combined potency of correct programming and perseverance is infallible. But early capitulation to initial negative feedback is simply a case of over-compensation which will have a negative effect.

Another source of danger which must be avoided at all costs is the negative activity of visualizing possible misadventures in the future. The person who allows negative pictures to infiltrate the screen of his or her mind is creating a very involved situation with all sorts of complex possibilities.

For example, suppose you think, 'What would happen to my family if I got cancer?' You would be embarking upon an intangible equation in which it is impossible to programme the situation. It can only be counter-productive to imagine those things which *may* happen. Visualize only that which definitely *will* happen or which actually *has* happened.

It is vitally important that you are very aware of the fact that, once you conjure up a picture in your mind, even if it is a fuzzy outline or a mere potential possibility, it becomes a reality as far as your brain is concerned. After all, Hypnothink is Hypnothink and programming is programming. Your brain-computer does not care about the difference between imagination and reality. That is the essence of Hypnothink.

We have already looked at how negative thoughts which slip unbidden into a Hypnothink visualization can be overcome – as in the case of Roseanne who wanted to take her little grandson for a walk in the park. But this occurred spontaneously during the course of a positive

Hypnothink. Don't create difficulties by asking yourself at the outset, 'But what if . . .'

REACTING TO STRESS STIMULI

Stress stimuli are far more powerful than you might imagine. Indeed, film-makers rely on this fact when they use particular sequences of images to evoke specific emotions in their audience. But while it might be quite entertaining to go along with the film-makers and experience nervous anticipation or semi-fear during a Hitchcock thriller and tearfulness during an old 'weepie', you do not want to allow yourself to be manipulated that way in real life.

Relationships

Vicky and Joe had been attracted to each other from the moment they first met. Over the next two or three months their relationship developed into an extremely passionate one. But after a while they realized that – however physically attracted to one another they might be – they had very little in common. In fact, as Vicky confided to her best friend, she wasn't even sure that she liked Joe very much. It wasn't that there was anything actually wrong with him – just that their tastes and interests were a million miles apart and they had very little to talk about to each other.

Finally the inevitable happened and the relationship got into difficulties. The main cause of this was Vicky's ever-increasing irritability with Joe – which he, for his part, was unable (or unwilling) to understand. But not being the most patient of young men, he was not prepared to tolerate the situation and so, having made his plans, he confronted Vicky one day with the fact that he had been offered a job in a town seventy miles away – a job which he fully intended to take. Having said that, he simply turned and left the room, the house and her life.

For a short time Vicky was numb and then she began to cry. Over the next few days she told her girlfriend that she was devastated by the way in which Joe had 'dumped' her. It was a cruel rejection and she was distraught. Then one day it struck her that she was not actually being true to her own emotions. All she was doing was acting in the way that a rejected lover was 'supposed' to act. After her confrontation with Joe, she had not stopped to think about what she felt or to question her emotional state. She had reacted to the stimulus of the situation and played her part the way life had programmed her to think it should be played.

So Vicky sat down and thought about how she really felt. She was, of course, sad – it is always sad when a relationship comes to an end. Her pride was bruised because she was the one who had been rejected – but not irreparably so. And she was furiously angry with Joe for the way in which he had acted – for being so underhand in making all the arrangements behind her back and then confronting her with the final outcome. She wished he could have been more open with her and told her what he was planning instead of leaving it until the day before he left town.

But if she was honest with herself, she was not really heartbroken that the relationship was over. Inwardly she had known for some time that it was not going to last for long. So why, she wondered, had she played the role of the distraught, abandoned lover? The simple answer is that she had reacted to one of life's stimuli without stopping to think. She had failed to let the doorbell ring.

Smoking

Perhaps one of the areas where this unthinking reaction to stress stimuli is most evident is among smokers. Someone trying to give up smoking has to deal with two main problems – apart from addiction to nicotine. These are the desire to smoke and the habit aspect. Of these, the desire is by far the easier to overcome. There may be many reasons why someone would *desire* to give up smoking – to improve their health, to prevent their family having to be passive smokers, to rid themselves of the unpleasant odour of stale tobacco, to save money or to be more acceptable socially. Habit, on the other hand, is another matter. The two main stimuli for smokers are:

Worry or anxiety

This type of smoker reacts negatively when under pressure or in a tense situation. You know the sort of thing – they have too many files on their desk so they reach for a cigarette. Or the telephone rings and, before even answering it, they pick up the packet of cigarettes.

'Social' occasions

So-called 'social smokers' may believe that they are not reacting to stress stimuli at all. After all, they tend to smoke during leisure time – in a pub or when out with a group of friends. And what about all those people who claim that the best cigarette is the one enjoyed after a meal?

What these people are doing, however, is betraying their own sense of inner insecurity. If they had a sufficiently high self-image, they would not need to rely on something artificial to help them enjoy a social situation. The pub or club smoker is really saying to the world, 'I need something to do with my hands so that I do not look or feel awkward.' The after-dinner smoker is demonstrating that he has so little confidence in his ability to be an interesting person that he needs the 'prop' of a cigarette to fill the gaps in what might otherwise be an awkward conversation.

If you are having difficulty in overcoming the habit aspect of smoking, Hypnothink can help you. Just be sure that, when practising your visualization, you imagine yourself without a cigarette in the type of situation which would normally cause you to smoke.

Health

Poor health – whether temporary or permanent – is naturally distressing. But so much depends upon what you are told and whether those words form a stress stimulus to which you react without stopping to let the doorbell ring.

The following is a true story from a time long before I was connected with hypnotherapy, Hypnothink, counselling or any of the other work I do now.

Within the space of one week I heard of two people I knew who had been diagnosed as having cancer. Both were middle-aged women. One was told that she had approximately three months to live, while the other was in hospital and so seriously ill that she was not expected to live for more than three weeks. The woman who was told that she had three months left, took to her bed and sat there waiting to die – and she did indeed die just three months later. The other woman, however, rallied and was sent home. She insisted that she was not ready to die and that she was not going to die. The cancer did not disappear but it did go into remission and she lived a further seven years. Not only that but she lived well and happily, enjoying life with her husband, her grown-up family and her friends.

The stress stimuli were the words of the respective doctors. They had actually specified lengths of time to the two women, though each had reacted differently. One had accepted the words of her doctor and given up hope, the other had paused and then found within herself a growing determination to live.

While I think that, on the whole, it is a good thing for doctors to be completely honest with their patients, I also think that the personality of the individual needs to be taken into account. Not everyone has the potential to be a fighter – and even this is often determined by past programming. The child who was either so dominated or so smothered that he was never able to develop a positive belief in himself is going to have such a poor self-image that he will automatically assume that any person he perceives as an authority figure *must* be right. Someone who has been allowed to develop a sense of self and a high self-esteem, however, will realize that, even if the authority figure is stating what they believe to be the absolute truth, no one is infallible and they just might be wrong. And this person will stop and think for themselves.

But you can change. Even if you grew up as a dominated or smothered child, you can become the person you want to be. None of us can change what happened to us in the past. But the one area over which we *do* have control is what we become in the future. If you use Hypnothink to help you to create a more positive self-image by changing your Inner Face, this will affect every area of your life – and could even help, in the long run, to prolong it or make it healthier.

USING HYPNOTHINK IN A POSITIVE RATHER THAN A NEGATIVE WAY

Every time you tell yourself that you 'can't' do something or every time you imagine something going wrong, you are effectively using Hypnothink. The trouble is that you are using it in a negative rather than a positive way. But look how successful it has been when used in a negative way: 'I can't speak to strangers . . . go in a lift . . . give up

smoking . . . go to the dentist . . . walk down the street.'
By saying such things to yourself over the years, you have
made them come true. If you can achieve so much in a
negative sense just by using the power of your own mind
– by Hypnothinking – surely you must be able to achieve
things positively, too.

When we looked at the case of Sandra and her phobia
about water, it was possible to see how the problem
had been comparatively small when it began, but had
increased in scope and intensity over the years.

Every time Sandra said to herself, 'I can't stand water',
or 'I can't go out in the rain', she had reinforced these
thoughts in her conscious and subconscious mind until
they became even more of a reality. More than that,
without realizing what she was doing, she had also
used the visualization aspect of Hypnothink (but in a
negative way) by imagining how dreadful it would be
and how terrible she would feel if she did, in fact, *do* one
of those things.

So, if you have until now been a negative thinker, you
can be assured that you will be extremely successful
using Hypnothink. You have been practising part of
the technique for years. All you have to do now is stop,
ignore the doorbell, and calmly and quietly work out
what you want to achieve and the positive visualization
to accompany these goals.

No one can take away the stress which accompanies modern-day living. But it is possible to eliminate
the harmful effects that the stress has upon you. Other
people may choose to react spontaneously to the stress
stimuli which surround them – but you do not have to.
You can choose to stop, relax and consider the circumstances before allowing yourself to react. You can let the
doorbell ring!

8

Get more living out of life

I don't suppose the person exists who does not want to improve his or her life in some way. And now you can do it. You can overcome your fears and achieve your goals. As long as you have a strong enough desire for the end result, all you then have to do is put the principles of Hypnothink into action.

NEGATIVE INFLUENCES

Sometimes, when applying those principles for the first time, people are troubled to find that negative thoughts keep intruding when they try to programme themselves positively – as was the case with Roseanne, the agoraphobic. These negative feelings emanate from your mind, not from some supernatural source – so you are quite entitled to dismiss them. Never give in to these negative influences. They can always be overcome. Anyone who gives in to such 'negatives' is displaying a lack of confidence in their own capabilities. You must be aggressive towards negative feelings. Think of them as a challenge to be overcome. In this instance, aggression – properly channelled – can be a source of additional strength. Passivity gives you nothing.

If you react positively to them, negative feelings need

not always be liabilities. For example, when a sports team is playing at home, the vocal support of its followers is an extremely potent force. In an away match, however, the team might confront the exact opposite – noisy hostility. But reacting aggressively to this hostility, the team could spur themselves on to even greater efforts. They could turn a negative influence to their own advantage and extract a positive result from it.

Every one of us has a personal 'gremlin' which seems to delight in popping negative thoughts into the mainstream of our thinking, but as Roseanne discovered, the answer is not to *not think* the negative thought – an impossibility – but to *outwit* it with a positive one. If you make it a habit to fill your mind with positive, desirable images, the negative ones will eventually evaporate. In a way you will be obeying the biblical injunction to overcome evil with good.

Worry

Worrying is a bad habit to get into. So many people practise worry until they become real experts at it. They think about the things which have gone wrong in the past and begin to apply those unpleasant memories and attitudes to the future. What they don't realize is that, by indulging in negative imagery from the past, they are in fact going a long way towards creating a negative future. To make matters worse, the chronic worrier then tries to make a conscious effort to 'stop worrying'. Of course, this doesn't work – and the failure merely creates even more tension. And tensions generate a worry-atmosphere.

What is the solution? The answer is to substitute pleasant wholesome images in the Inner Face. These will overwhelm and erase any negative ones – the worry images. Try going a stage further and create an attitude of mind in which, whenever a negative image occurs, it triggers a good image which contributes to a positive state of mind. Use your negative images as a response stimulator. It is far easier than you think.

Editing your past

Your brain can be compared to a tape recorder with some good stories with happy endings and some sad stories with unhappy endings. The brain is made up of tens of thousands of ingredients from your past experience. You can juggle these ingredients as you wish. Remember a broadcasting company edits its tapes. So can you. Cut out the bits you don't like, change the story line, add some extra bits, make yourself the hero! There is no limit to the imagery you can choose. You can do whatever you like.

Hypnothink offers you freedom from any past influences which may have adversely affected your present life. You no longer have to be tied down by the character formed during your childhood. In terms of the Hypnothink concept, your character is changeable, modifiable – even replaceable.

Contemporary psychology tends to hold extremely pessimistic theories – for example, that most people are bent on self-destruction in one form or another. Hypnothink liberates us from these self-imposed shackles. It gives us access to true human dignity – which means that there is no longer any need to be a helpless victim of unfortunate circumstances. You can assume responsibility for your own future. No one is trying to make you pretend that your past did not exist, but now you can cope with that past, conquer the present and make plans for the future.

THE LINK BETWEEN MIND AND BODY

There is undoubtedly a link between one's state of mind (or attitude to life) and one's state of body (physical condition). Complementary medicine advocates the philosophy of holistic therapy in which the body's own defence mechanism is stimulated to overcome physical problems.

There is a wonderful power which flows through all of us – a Life Force. Great men in medicine and philosophy through the ages have recognized its existence, but have differed in their definition of it. Freud called it Drive; Jung called it Libido; Pierre Janet termed it Mental Energy. It is not being flippant simply to think of it as Mental Energy. And the more you have of this whatever-it-is, the more resistant you are to disease and the younger you will feel. Even physical injuries – from minor cuts and grazes to much more serious problems – will heal far more quickly. This state of 'Feeling Good' is the opposite of the state of mind mentioned earlier in which gloom predominates and the mood is down instead of up.

Just as a positive attitude can have a direct organic effect on the body, so can a negative state of mind be a liability – and perhaps much more. Research conducted at the University of Rochester's Medical Center in New York explored the mental states of forty patients who were about to undergo clinical tests to establish whether or not they were suffering from cancer. Of those forty, fourteen patients confessed to having feelings of hopelessness, while the other twenty-six said they were not experiencing such feelings. Of the fourteen who felt hopeless, no fewer than nine proved to have cancer. Of the twenty-six who did not feel hopeless, only three had cancer. Dr A.H. Schmale, the physician connected with the research, is on record as observing that 'the subconscious awareness of a malignant growth is within the realms of possibility'.

The psychosomatic link has been examined still further by Dr Samuel Silverman, American psychoanalyst and Associate Professor of Psychiatry at the Harvard Medical School. After thirty years of research, he believes that all illnesses are probably the result of interaction between the emotions and the body.

While he was analysing patients, Dr Silverman noticed that dreams, fears and personal associations sometimes prefigure physical diseases. One woman produced a whole range of thoughts and hints – including a dream in which she rode in a red car with a German Shepherd dog. The woman soon afterwards developed German measles – the symptom of which is a red rash.

An even more astonishing example of this potent mind/body link was provided by a guilt-ridden professor. This man had a bad sexual relationship with his wife. He also hated his father – to such an extent that he actively wished for his death. His father had serious problems with his eyesight. In flight from his domestic sexual problems, the professor became a voyeur, reading pornography and watching sex exhibitions. Dr Silverman reported that the burden of guilt created by these associations resulted in the professor developing critical eyesight problems. As a result of detached retinas, he later became almost blind.

In four cases reported in his book, *Psychological Clues in Forecasting Physical Illness*, (Butterworth and Appleton, 1971) Dr Silverman successfully predicted just when, after severe prolonged stress, illness would come – and which part of the body would suffer.

One successful prediction of imminent respiratory disease came after a patient said that his girlfriend's heavy smoking reminded him of his mother, who had died of a chronic respiratory ailment. A further clue was that he had dreamed of a nearly forgotten girlfriend and casually mentioned chest pains he had once suffered when involved in a car accident with her.

Dr Silverman asserts that the answer to the question of whether illness is emotionally caused is that it is caused by the interaction of mind and body. As he says, 'The clues are psychological as well as physical.'

When a person develops critical stress and cannot cope,

either the mind or the body has to break down. And should it be a physical illness that strikes us, it does so not at random but at vulnerable spots unique to each of us.

An oblique testimony to the effectiveness of the right kind of thinking is provided by the use of placebos in medical research. A placebo, of course, is a harmless substitute passed off by the doctor as an effective medicine. They are used when working with a control group: nine patients might receive, for example, a new vaccine and the tenth will receive a placebo – not knowing that it is actually a neutral substance.

It is an established medical fact that placebos often work. The patient thinks and believes that he has been given a valid and effective medicine. The result is that his condition improves. Medical researchers tend to dismiss the effect of placebos as 'suggestion' – but this is not really the explanation. A placebo works because it arouses the expectation of improvement in the mind of the patient – the fact of future good health is created in the mind.

In his book *Mind Over Body*, Dr Vernon Coleman (Guild Publishing, 1989) states: 'The evidence which shows the extent of the human body's healing powers is impressive enough, but this is only the beginning. There is now increasing evidence to show that our health is influenced not just by what we eat or how much exercise we take, and not just by our own bodies' internal protective mechanisms, but by our attitudes, our expectations, our hopes, our moods, our personalities and our temperaments. Our health is not just influenced by physical forces but by mental forces too – and these mental forces are far more powerful and have a far greater effect on our health than any other factor.'

Some years ago I had as a patient a young woman in her early twenties – I'll call her Pauline. Once again I was a 'last resort' for someone who had already been from doctor to consultant to hospital to psychiatrist before coming to see me. After thorough and extensive check-ups, each of these people had told her that they could find nothing wrong with her physically. And yet, as she insisted to me through tears of frustration, she *knew* that she was not well. She could not tell me how this 'not well' manifested itself other than that she felt permanently listlessness and lacking in energy.

I asked Pauline how long she had been feeling like this and she claimed that it was for at least five years. Through hypnosis I took her back to a time, five years earlier in her life, to see if we could find any clue as to what had happened.

Five years earlier Pauline had her appendix removed – a simple operation from which she had recovered speedily and fully. Under hypnosis it was possible to return to the time of that surgery – even back to the time in the operating theatre itself.

As Pauline had neither been able to see what was going on nor to experience any pain during the operation (having, of course, been anaesthetized), she was not able to see anything or to feel pain while hypnotized. But she did tell me that she could *hear* what was going on at the time.

Hypnotherapists have long held that those under anaesthetic can still hear what is going on around them. And, to give them their due, some members of the medical profession are now coming round to that way of thinking.

During surgery Pauline heard two nurses talking. At one point one of the nurses said to the other, 'I think we're going to lose her.' The other replied, 'Even if she survives, she'll never be quite right.'

Now Pauline *had* survived and subsequent check-ups had shown that she was 'quite right' physically. However, somewhere in her subconscious was the conviction that this could not be the case – and so her body had chosen to comply with her inner belief, leaving her with this sensation of being permanently unwell.

Fortunately we were able to go back to Pauline's consultant and explain the situation. He confirmed that there had indeed been an unexpected and serious problem during the operation itself but that this had been completely overcome. He showed Pauline her X-rays and her medical notes and she was at last convinced that this was the truth of the matter. From that day onwards Pauline no longer felt 'unwell'.

AGEING

Hypnothink can affect the ageing process too. 'You are as old as you feel' is not just a meaningless cliché. The generally accepted attitude nowadays seems to be that middle age is the period between forty and fifty-five. Much younger people are sometimes inclined to write off anyone over thirty. This is a deplorably negative – and inaccurate – attitude. How much more desirable it would be – and how much more beneficial to the human race – if the concept of 'middle age' were to change to incorporate the period from, say, seventy upwards.

As one young fifty-year-old woman, who was well used to the principles of Hypnothink, put it: 'Middle-aged people are always those who are at least ten years older than I am.'

It is amazing how many people automatically give themselves a life expectancy equivalent to that of their parents. A great many anxiety neuroses arise from a fear of death which is based on the knowledge that the sufferer is reaching the age at which his or her parents died. This is, of course, a quite unfounded fear.

In John Schindler's admirable book, *How to Live 365 Days a Year* he enumerates the needs of human beings as follows:

- love
- security
- creative experience
- recognition
- new experiences
- self-esteem

I would add one more to that list – the need to be able to look forward to the future with happy anticipation. One must have somewhere to go – something to aim for.

There are countless examples of people who retire at sixty-five and are dead by sixty-six. Yet others keep on working and remain active into their nineties. Goethe was over eighty when he wrote *Faust*. Edison was still active in his nineties. Picasso was still painting well when he was eighty. The great British actress. Dame Edith Evans, was doing an arduous one-woman show when in her eighties. A. E. Matthews was acting in the West End of London when he died – well into his nineties.

This doesn't necessarily mean that you should fight frantically against retirement when the appropriate time comes. What is does mean is that you should look on that retirement as the beginning of the next phase of your life rather than the ending of the last one. Particularly today, when most people have a long life expectancy after the age of sixty-five, it would be foolish, depressing – and physically harmful – to consider the useful part of your life as having come to an end.

Your mental attitude, of course, can have a great effect on your physical appearance. It is often very true to say that if you act and really feel young, you are more likely to retain a youthful appearance.

Some women can fall victim to a negative response when they are either divorced or widowed. I have known women in such situations who have regarded their lives as over – and let themselves 'grow old' as a result. I have known many others who have regarded the setback – however unhappy it made them at the time – as a challenge. Those who respond in the latter way will deliberately set out to make new lives for themselves – including, if they want them, new relationships – and this setting out acts as a spur and a stimulus. Their personalities seem to blossom. They both look and behave younger. And because of their attitude and reactions, they find the new lives they are seeking.

It is really sad when you see people who retire from their jobs taking the attitude that they have not only retired from work, but also from life. Such people tend to describe themselves as 'worn out'. They say that they feel as though they are just 'hanging on'. They have created for themselves an Inner Face which shows them as being physically and mentally expended, merely holding on to life with their fingertips. Naturally, the result is that unless they learn to change the way they think, they soon lose that grip on life.

One of the most irritating clichés must be, 'You can't teach an old dog new tricks.' What nonsense! Of course you can – provided the 'old dog' is willing to learn.

I have had the most wonderful and satisfying results with elderly patients who were co-operative and prepared to use their imaginative abilities.

Naturally these people have a rich and varied stock of experiences on which to draw when using Hypnothink. After all, they have lived for more years. One man, well into his seventies, was helped to overcome a stammer he had had since the age of four. And many, many patients in their seventies and eighties have overcome a wide variety of ailments.

ATTAINING WISDOM

Surely our goal must be to get more living out of life. To achieve this we must accept whatever wisdom we can derive from any source – whether it be science, religion, psychology or the areas of mysticism.

New knowledge in psychology often comes from non-medical sources. It is sometimes only those on the outside who are most able to take a truly fresh look at things. Freud asserted that there must be non-medical psychologists, because people who had been trained within that particular discipline tended to propagate the teachings of those from whom they had learned. This, he claimed, would naturally lead to a somewhat restricted view.

Think of some of the world's famous 'outsiders'. Pasteur was not a medical man yet he invented the process of pasteurization. The Wright brothers, the first men to fly, were bicycle manufacturers. Einstein was a mathematician, not a physicist. Curie was not a qualified doctor.

There is no doubt that we all have certain powers which are presently inexplicable, and in a sense it is these powers that we tap into when practising Hypnothink. This technique can teach each and every one of us how to modify our own personality and tune in to success and contentment for the rest of our lives.

MAKING CHANGES

One of the most important stages in making changes in yourself is to give yourself permission to make them. It is part of human nature to want to cling on to what we already know and have experienced. Change, by its very nature, can be frightening because you are never quite sure what you are going to find at the end of the road.

Yet, if you were to say to almost anyone, 'Do you really want to change?', they would probably look at you in amazement. 'Of course I do,' they would say. 'Do you think I *like* living with this problem?' The answer, in fact, is not that they like it but that they have become used to it. They may not be happy – but at least it is an unhappiness they are familiar with and they know its boundaries. To turn around and face in a new direction when you don't know where that road is going to lead can be terrifying. The conscious mind can list all the logical reasons for making changes but the subconscious mind will put up a pretty good argument against most of them.

Think back to when you were a child. There came a

day when you took the stabilizers off your first bicycle and wobbled along the path. You were a bit scared – but you were exhilarated, too. And what about the time when you finally had to let go of the handrail or the pole to which you had been clinging in the swimming bath and just go for it on your own. That was also frightening – but, oh, that wonderful moment when you realized that you were actually swimming by yourself!

Making up your mind not simply to regret the problems around and within you but to get out there and make an effort to change things is also frightening. But there is nothing to compare with the day you succeed. So think it over and then give yourself permission to make those changes. Say it aloud if you like. Or write a contract with yourself. Formalize this permission and you will be going part of the way to releasing yourself from the bondage of the past.

Some people put off making changes because they decide that it's 'better the devil you know'. In other words, if they have coped with their problem until now, they think they will be able to go on coping with it – even if they are not happy with it – in the future. But they are wrong. If you don't make an effort to make things better, you are not going to remain as you are. Any therapist – and most sufferers – will tell you that if a particular condition is not dealt with, it does not remain static but gets worse.

Just as Sandra began by not wanting to swim or immerse herself in water, she eventually reached the stage where she could not tolerate even the smallest amount of it – where it ruined her life until she did something about overcoming it. In the same way, many other people who begin with small manifestations of symptoms with which they feel able to cope, eventually find themselves being overwhelmed by a mass of symptoms with which they cannot cope. Let's look at some typical examples:

Arthur had always been of a nervous disposition and as the years went on he began to suffer anxiety attacks. These did not seem to follow any particular pattern and so he never knew when one would come upon him.

The symptoms associated with these attacks would be the feeling that his heart was 'racing', a sense of giddiness and the feeling that he was going to pass out altogether (although he never did).

Eventually Arthur became so frightened of having one of these unpleasant attacks that he was forever 'monitoring' himself. He would lie in bed at night listening to the beating of his heart and trying to tell whether or not it was becoming more rapid. And, of course, one of the things that happened was that the very fear of this occurring actually *made* Arthur's heart beat more quickly. And so a vicious circle was created whereby fear of having an attack actually caused it to happen – and this in turn caused him to become even more fearful and even more watchful afterwards.

Elizabeth was an asthmatic. She had suffered from this distressing condition since childhood. Now it is an established fact that, whatever the primary cause of the asthma, it is always made worse by stress or tension.

Even if you are fortunate enough never to have suffered from asthma, you will know that an attack is extremely distressing for the sufferer who finds him or herself fighting for every breath.

All asthmatics get an 'early warning signal'. They know when an attack is about to occur. What usually happens then – and what certainly happened in Elizabeth's case – was that the fear and dread of the impending attack made her even more tense as she tried to hold it at bay. But, of course, the very tension caused by this internal fight, precipitated and increased the attack itself.

Elizabeth found, as many asthmatics do, that as the years passed her attacks became stronger and more frequent, and she felt increasingly powerless to do anything about it.

Yet, had she been able to deliberately relax as soon as she had an inkling that an attack was pending, all Elizabeth would have been left with was her 'early warning signal', with which she could easily have coped. Martin suffered from insomnia. It had begun when he was going through a particularly stressful time at work, where people around him were being made redundant and he feared for the security of his own job. But even after the situation had improved and he knew that his job was safe, the insomnia persisted. It had by then become a habit.

Night after night Martin would go to bed thinking 'I'm so tired. I do hope I can get some sleep tonight.' And night after night he would lie there, watching the luminous hands of the bedside clock as they marked the passing hours, growing more and more frustrated as he realized that, even if he were to fall asleep, he would not be getting his full quota and would probably feel dreadful in the morning.

Martin tried everything he could think of. Sometimes he had a stiff drink before retiring but he found that, although he would fall asleep quite quickly, he would be awake again in the early hours and would lie there tossing and turning until it was time to get up. Sometimes he watched television until very late, hoping that by then he would be so tired that he would sleep easily. But, of course, late night television programmes are often the most violent or the most stimulating and so, tired as he was, when he went to bed his mind was racing and he was unable to sleep at all.

TAKING YOUR MIND OFF THE PROBLEM

All three of the people mentioned above actually made their problems worse because they concentrated upon them. What they really needed to do was to fill their minds with something else and thereby avoid the situation they most feared.

We are only capable of thinking one thought at a time. Even when we think we are doing two things at once – perhaps reading a magazine and listening to the radio – our minds are actually skipping from one to the other. So it follows that if you fill your mind with a specific thought or visualization, it is not possible to be worrying about your current problem.

Here's how the three people mentioned learned to help themselves with Hypnothink:

- Arthur used the 'special place' technique. When he felt himself beginning to grow anxious, instead of monitoring his heartbeat, he sat in his chair or lay in bed and practised the basic Hypnothink technique before taking himself in his imagination to a spot he found both beautiful and relaxing.

  We had chosen this 'place' quite carefully when Arthur had come to see me. The criteria were that (a) it had to be a place which would appeal to him in reality and (b) I wanted him to be able to incorporate some steady rhythmic sounds into the imagined scene. Arthur told me that he loved the sea, and so he chose a visualization which involved him lying on a soft towel on a white sandy beach. He was shaded from the heat of the sun by a huge umbrella but he could feel the warmth of the air relaxing his muscles and could hear the gentle, rhythmic sound of the waves on the shore.

  The reason for incorporating the sound in Arthur's case was that, provided he concentrated fully on his imagined scene, his heartbeat would slow itself in order to keep time with that steady rhythm. Thus all possibility of a panic attack would disappear.

- When Elizabeth received her 'early warning signal' of an approaching asthma attack, she, too, had to stop what she was doing and take the time to relax and visualize. At first she said that if she was at work, for example, she could not just stop. But as I pointed out to her, if she did not and if the attack actually took hold, she would lose far more working time and cause far more disruption in the office than if she took a few moments to make the attack go away.

Once again, the specific visualization will vary according to the preferences of the patient. But the one Elizabeth eventually decided to use was one which is effective for many asthmatics.

At the first sign of an impending attack, Elizabeth would sit or lie down and concentrate on relaxing her body. She then visualized two balloons behind her ribs, and as she breathed in and out she would imagine these two balloons inflating and deflating. By concentrating on inflating the balloons as fully as possible, she was automatically taking as much air into her lungs as possible. As soon as she was breathing well, the threat of the attack would always pass.

This did not make Elizabeth someone who was no longer an asthmatic. What it did do was make her someone who was fully in control of her condition. She never again needed to suffer anything more than a few early indications that an attack might be approaching. In fact, as her confidence grew in her own ability to control the situation, even these early signs became less and less frequent.

Martin had already discovered that you cannot *make* yourself fall asleep. Probably one of the most unfortunate phrases in the English language is 'go to sleep'. It implies that you have to *do* something in order to sleep. Whereas, in fact, if you can relax and take your mind off the time, filling it with other thoughts, sleep will come to you.

Martin was a garden lover and so we used a visualization which made use of this fact. After practising the basic Hypnothink technique, he would take himself in his imagination to a truly beautiful garden. He imagined that he was lying on a luxuriously comfortable sun-lounger looking around this garden, which was ablaze with colour in the summer sun.

The visualization continued with Martin – still on his comfortable chair – watching the way the garden changed as the day went on and light began to fade. He imagined how it would be in late afternoon when long fingers of shadow stretched across the grass and the colours of the flowers were more muted, then at dusk when the garden was quieter and more tranquil. Finally he imagined it at night when only the palest flowers could be seen among the dark shadows of the trees and shrubs.

By following this visualization, Martin was taking his mind away from all thoughts of whether or not he would be able to sleep and concentrating on something he found pleasurable. At the same time, his subconscious was accepting that he was 'shutting down' as the day came to an end, and because he was so relaxed, sleep came naturally to him.

HYPNOTHINK AND SERIOUS ILLNESS

Hypnothink is also extremely effective when dealing with more serious health conditions. You will remember that the technique was originally devised as a result of Romark's stroke, and there have been a considerable number of successes since then with other stroke victims.

Molly was a sweet and gentle lady in her late sixties. Some six months before I first met her she had suffered a stroke from which she had partially recovered. She now had no problems with her speech, but her movements were slow and she found walking extremely difficult. In fact she could only manage to walk around her bungalow with the aid of two walking sticks.

It was this inability to walk which distressed Molly

more than anything. She had good friends who helped her by doing her shopping but she really missed being able to go out to buy the occasional item. Even more, she missed taking her little dog to the park for their regular afternoon walk – something she had not been able to do since her stroke.

In spite of all her problems, Molly was a positive and determined person. She learned the techniques of Hypnothink and practised them well. Although it took several weeks, during which time she also had some sessions of physiotherapy, by the end of her course of treatment she was once again able to get out and about. True, she still had a slight limp which would probably never leave her. She also used a single walking stick when she went out as this gave her an added sense of security – although she discarded it completely when indoors. But she had achieved her ambition – she could now take her dog to the park, she could go to the local corner shop and she could walk down the road to visit her friend.

Many cancer patients also benefit from techniques such as Hypnothink. Indeed, most of the cancer centres and clinics have come to use visualization as part of the treatment offered. Hypnothink simply provides a method of harnessing and intensifying the visualization and speeding the link between the subconscious mind and the physical body.

At no time would I suggest that patients suffering from cancer or any other life-threatening disease use Hypnothink *instead* of whatever orthodox or complementary medical treatment they might be having. It is, however, a wonderful addition to such treatment and has often enhanced and accelerated it.

TEACHING OTHERS

Although this book is written to show *you* how you can employ the technique of Hypnothink to improve your own life, it is also possible to teach the techniques to those you care for in order to help them solve whatever problems might be bothering them. Many people who have come to me seeking help in overcoming their own problems have gone on to use the same methods to help their children at different phases of their lives.

Children today are under great pressure to succeed. And this now seems to begin at a far earlier age. Perhaps because parents are so aware of the difficulty of obtaining work, even for those who go on to further education, they are very anxious for their children to do well at school in order to give themselves the best possible chance in the future. And as they grow up, the children themselves are all too aware of the problems which may lie ahead of them as they try to make their way in the world.

This combination leads to a great deal of pressure being experienced by schoolchildren and students, particularly at exam time. Even those who have studied and revised can be so overcome by this pressure that they are unable to think clearly when taking exams and allow their nervousness to become dominant so that they do not acquit themselves as well as they should.

Hypnothink can counteract these 'nerves'. It cannot, of course, replace the hard work and studying which the students must do, but it can prevent them letting themselves down at the most important times simply because of pressure and anxiety.

There are, in addition, many ways in which these children and students can be helped to make learning and revising simpler and more effective. This has the added benefit of increasing their self-confidence – which also helps when they are being examined or tested. And it is not only in the area of studying that children experience crises of confidence. Shyness and nervousness are not the prerogative of the adult world.

One of my patients, Rachel, was concerned about Penny, her fifteen-year-old daughter. Although a bright and lively girl, Penny had never lost her childhood shyness. Indeed it had grown worse (as we have seen that these things do) as she grew older.

Penny was quite comfortable with the immediate family or when in the company of her best friend Lauren. But as soon as a situation called for her to be among a group – even a comparatively small one – she would become tongue-tied and would stand silently on the edge of the gathering, blushing furiously if anyone addressed her.

Because she had learned about Hypnothink when dealing with problems of her own. Rachel was able to teach them to Penny, thereby helping her. The girl did not suddenly become the 'life and soul of the party' – that simply was not her nature. But she achieved what she wanted, which was to be able to mix comfortably with a group of her peers.

Similar techniques can be used to help the elderly who may feel that their usefulness has come to an end. Once someone has been helped to find a direction in life – and that need is just as valid at seventy as it is at seventeen – then life becomes meaningful again. Thus a benign (as opposed to vicious) circle is created. The individual concerned develops interests and involvements which make them a more interesting person to know. As a result of this, they find that others are more likely to seek out their company and so their confidence and their belief in themselves as a worthwhile person with a great deal to offer is fostered.

Since Hypnothink first came about in the 1970s, literally thousands of people have been helped by the technique. Many of these asked how they could pass this knowledge on to people overseas or help other people that they knew. So, in the early 1980s, the Hypnothink Course was created. By means of written text (requiring written work in return) and recorded cassette, people all over the world have been taught how to reprogramme themselves for success. While some of these people have been more than content to see the changes taking place in their own lives, others have gone on to take the necessary examination to allow them to become qualified Hypnothink Counsellors, recognized and registered as such. (Details of how to find out about this course can be found in the Appendix at the back of the book.)

9

Be a people-person

The foundations for the way you relate to people throughout your life are laid very early on – certainly long before you are able to speak or rationalize, and possibly even before you are born.

By means of hypnosis it is quite possible to take someone back to the time when they were still in their mother's womb – although usually to the later rather than the earlier months. And although the unborn child does not understand the actual words spoken, it certainly is aware of atmosphere and emotion. So, whether the general feeling is one of peace and harmony or fear and anger, the unborn baby absorbs it and it becomes part of the nature with which he or she is born.

Once a child is born, there is no doubt that he or she will learn subconsciously from the adults who are around at the time. A nervous parent will create nervousness in the child, just as a placid one will create an aura of peace. This arises even though the child has not had the time – nor the ability – to work out just what has caused this nervousness or sense of tranquillity.

From then on the influence is more obvious. Parents who have a fear of dogs ... or noise ... or people ... are likely to pass on this fear to their child, even if they try hard not to do so. A mother or father who is undemonstrative is likely to raise an undemonstrative child – however desperately that child may be silently yearning for obvious signs of love. The adult may be able to look back and say, 'I know my mother loved me and that she demonstrated that love every time she cooked me a meal or bought me a present', but the child will have been aware that physical demonstrations of love were missing and may well have interpreted the situation – albeit wrongly – as meaning that the love did not exist in the first place.

All these things happen when the child has no control over what is going on and how people are behaving. His first Inner Face will be formed by other people and his reaction to them. Fortunately, as you have already seen, this does not have to be his Inner Face for the rest of his life. When he is old enough to realize what has happened and how his insecurities have come about, he will be able to use Hypnothink to alter his self-perception and help him to become the person he really wants to be.

If only it were possible for all new parents to be told how their behaviour affects the self-esteem of their child as it grows. (And when my children were young I was no wiser than most other parents – there are so many things I would do differently knowing what I do now.) It is actually within our power to create a generation of positive, confident, children – if we but knew it at the right time.

HELPING YOUR CHILDREN WITH HYPNOTHINK

However, all is not lost. For one thing, as those children grow to adulthood and become aware of techniques such as Hypnothink, they can make use of them in order to improve and enhance their own lives. For another, even if your children are part grown, there is still time for you to help them and improve their Inner Face at this highly important and impressionable time.

Any child above the age of seven or eight can be taught

how to use Hypnothink – although the development of the relevant visualization, and ensuring the regular practice of the technique, may well require a certain amount of input from the parent. And if a child learns how to use Hypnothink at a very early age, he or she will be able to keep that knowledge stored away until required for further use at some later stage of life. Just knowing that you have the means of putting things right for yourself is often enough to give the self-confidence needed to prevent many of life's emotional problems arising in the first place.

Linda was a young, divorced mother with one small daughter, upon whom she doted. Becky had been a shy and somewhat clinging child for the whole of her young life. From the age of three she had attended a local playgroup in the village hall. There she had played quite contentedly with the toys – and occasionally with another child – provided she knew that her mother was sitting at the far end of the room. But on the rare occasion when Linda decided to leave her daughter there for an hour or so while she popped out to do some shopping, Becky had become really distressed and sobbed in a corner, running to cling to her mother when she returned. Not wanting to upset her daughter, Linda had arranged her daily life so that she could always be present during playgroup sessions.

As the time approached for Becky to go to 'big school', Linda grew very worried. She could not sit in the corner of the classroom every day. How was she to persuade Becky to stay without her – and to stay happily, making her own contribution to the class?

At only five years of age, Becky was a little younger than most of the children I have worked with. But when Linda came to see me, we decided to use a modified version of Hypnothink to help the little girl overcome her anxiety.

First Linda had to talk to Becky about the school she was going to, emphasizing how much fun it was going to be, the kind of activities she would be able to take part in and how much she was going to enjoy herself. Into each of these conversations Linda built phrases such as 'And when I come to collect you in the afternoon, we'll have tea together and you can tell me all about it', or 'If you paint a picture for me, I'll hang it on the kitchen wall where everyone who comes to the house can see it.'

In this way Becky grew used to the idea that:

- She was definitely going to school – at no time did Linda ask her whether she would like to go; it was simply given as an accepted fact.
- There would be plenty to do, particularly painting which she really enjoyed.
- Her mother would collect her every afternoon and take her home – with the unspoken inference that she would not be staying at the school to keep an eye on her.
- There would be things for her to tell her mother when she got home – in other words, this would be a part of her life in which her mother was not involved.

Because Linda started to talk like this when September was still a long way off, Becky did not feel the need to become anxious about the prospect of going to school in the autumn.

During the preceding summer term. Linda made arrangements to take Becky to have a look at the school and to see the classroom she would be using. She made sure that she showed her daughter where the toilets were, where coats and outdoor shoes were to be kept, where she would go to eat and – most importantly – the gate where she would meet her after school every single day.

During that time, too, Linda began to use a form of Hypnothink with Becky. Every night, when the little girl was in bed, Linda would get her to pretend that she was very heavy and floppy. Then she described to Becky the wheel and explained that it was a 'magic wheel' and that when you passed through the centre of it, you were in a special place where everything

happened just as you wanted it. A child's imagination
is a wonderful thing, knowing no bounds, so Becky
was quite happy to go along with this new form of
bedtime story.

Linda would then continue by describing to Becky the
scene as she went into school in the morning, looked at
the books in the classroom or played in the playground
at lunch time. She made the scenes as happy and as
detailed as possible, incorporating such things as the
coloured ribbon Becky would be wearing in her hair,
the new pencils she would have in her bag and the
cuddles they would have when she met her mother at
the gate in the afternoon. She also made sure that she
described in detail the areas of the school Becky had
already seen.

Although Becky was too young to have worked through
the visualization process on her own, a child's imagination is such that, if someone else is describing something to her, she will automatically picture it in her
mind.

This was, I suppose, a form of 'assisted Hypnothink' –
and it worked extremely well. It had the added advantage
that it fulfilled the 'last thing at night' criterion. These
positive descriptions of how life was going to be at
school were the last thing Becky heard before going to
sleep each night. Thus she had the whole night for her
subconscious to work on these images and she would
wake in the morning with positive and happy thoughts
about her future still in her mind.

By the time the great day came and Becky was to
be taken to school for the first time, her subconscious
had grown so used to the ideas and the images which
accompanied them, that it did not occur to her to do other
than look forward to the day ahead. There was the briefest
of anxious moments when mother and daughter had to
say goodbye to each other at the school gate, but Becky
soon turned and went through the door with nothing
more than a brief wave.

If you have a child who is too young to be able to practise Hypnothink alone, then you can do as Linda did and turn it into a bedside story with your own child as the hero or heroine.

Praise and credit are essential to any boy or girl who thinks that he or she has done something praiseworthy. So, when your child successfully carries out that which he or she has been imagining, let them know you have noticed and that you are proud of them. Nothing breeds self-confidence as quickly as the knowledge that someone else not only has great confidence in you but is proud of you for what you have done.

Working with your child in this way has another great benefit. It allows you to spend quality time together and, however many children you have, at that particular instant the son or daughter you are working with is aware that they have your undivided attention – something every child cherishes.

As the child becomes a teenager, Hypnothink can prove even more useful. The teenage years are difficult ones in so many ways and each adolescent needs all the help he or she can get. Whether we are talking about schoolwork, general shyness or difficulties in forming the right kind of relationships with the opposite sex, there has never been as much pressure on our teenage sons and daughters as there appears to be today.

Not so many years ago, pupils who did reasonably well at school knew that they would be able to find a job. That is no longer the case, as many of those in their late teens will confirm – even those who have gone on to further education. So the pressure upon them seems to be even greater, and from an even earlier age. Parents and teachers often urge them to work hard so that they might do well in their exams – or how do they ever expect to get a job? They hear from their own friends of older brothers and sisters who have been unable to find work after leaving school. So the stress is present at a far earlier age and to a far greater extent than used to be the case.

At the same time, pressure to be a 'grown-up' is also increasing. Pass the playground of any school and you can see these nine- and ten-year old mini-men and women and listen to them talking about their boyfriends and girlfriends. I actually knew of one child of nine who was distraught because, as she told her mother, she was the only one in her class without a special boyfriend.

Whether or not we like these examples of junior man and womanhood, the fact remains that no child likes to seem different from its peers. Consequently children will either go out of their way to conform or become rebellious in an attempt to prove that they 'don't really care'.

If you are to help your children and your teenagers, they need to know right from the very beginning that you are there for them to talk to. A child who can confide in one or both parents is far less likely to suffer from juvenile stress. Even if there are occasions when you feel there is little you can do in a practical sense, the fact that you have been there, giving them time, listening to them and understanding their viewpoint will be of assistance in releasing some of that pressure.

No one is expecting you to be always sweetness and light – in fact it would be wrong to be so. A child needs to know that its parents are human beings, capable of being happy or sad, easy-going or irritable. How else will he or she grow up to know what real life is like? An ideal world would be filled with people who were always smiling, always good-humoured and who always did the right thing – but this is not an ideal world and all we can do is strive to do the best we can as often as we can. So, while our children need to know that we are trying our best, it is no bad thing for them to realize that we also slip from time to time.

For all children, stress levels increase at exam time. In my book *Memory Power* (Vermillion 1993), I describe methods of thinking and learning creatively so that the whole process is more fun and much easier. When it comes to the exams themselves, Hypnothink can be an enormous help.

One of the reasons for the terror with which many people regard exams is that they are comparatively rare – perhaps once a term or twice within the academic year. By using Hypnothink and regularly visualizing the exam set-up prior to the actual event, it becomes 'ordinary' so far as the subconscious mind is concerned, and thus the level of stress associated with it is reduced. Naturally there is still revision to be done. No one is going to pass any exam if they do not know the subject. But most of those who do really badly in exams do not fail because of lack of knowledge but because of lack of confidence – or 'exam nerves'.

There are so many ways in which you can use Hypnothink and allied techniques to help your children as they grow. The older ones can be taught what to do and left to get on with it while the younger ones will require positive input from you. Wouldn't it be wonderful if we could create a generation of individuals with self-confidence and a positive self-image . . . a really healthy Inner Face.

RELATING TO OTHERS

There are many people whose self-esteem is not high when they are with other people. Sometimes this results in shyness, sometimes in verbal – or even physical – aggression. Sometimes sufferers feel so bad about themselves that they do what they can to avoid contact with other people altogether.

These Inner Faces have not descended from the ether; they have been formed by people and circumstances in the life of the person with low self-esteem. But, just as you can record over an old audio or video tape, you can superimpose a new Inner Face which will, at the same time, remove all traces of the old one.

If you are able to understand *why* your poor Inner Face arose and who or what caused it in the first place, there is quite a simple technique you can practise to nullify the harmful effect of that earlier event. Let's look at a common example taken from my own case files.

Sibling rivalry

Fran was the oldest of three children. She had a brother just two years younger than herself and a little sister nearly ten years younger. Fran's parents probably loved all three children but they both − and the mother in particular − doted upon the youngest. This little girl was exceptionally pretty and also went on to do very well at school.

Fran was also good-looking but in her early teens did not believe this to be the case. And however hard she worked and however much she tried to please, she never seemed to get more than a B for her schoolwork. (Little sister, of course, was being given one A after another.)

Fran was naturally jealous although she tried not to show it. Her mother, however, made the situation far worse by always comparing the two girls. 'Why can't you be like your sister?' eventually turned to 'Oh, you're useless' or 'Can't you do anything right?'

I did not meet Fran until she was in her early thirties, by which time her self-esteem had plummeted to the greatest depths. No matter where she went or what she did, she never really believed that she had anything to offer. Her mother's words had created an all too powerful effect.

This is what we did to counteract the words, deeds and thoughts of the past:

1. First Fran had to sit quietly and relax as well as she possibly could.
2. Next she had to imagine she was in a darkened cinema. On the screen was a typical scene from her own childhood – one where her mother was belittling her or comparing her unfavourably with her little sister.
3. When she felt the time was right – at the moment of greatest hurt – I told Fran to 'freeze' the picture on her imaginary screen.
4. Now she had to study that picture. What was the little girl (Fran as a child) thinking and feeling?
5. Next I told Fran the adult to get into the picture between her mother and the child she used to be. Defending the child and its position in a way she would never have had the courage to do at the time, Fran was to let rip and say anything she wished to the mother. She then had to reassure the child that she was loved and understood.
6. Now she could unfreeze the picture and allow the scene to continue. But this time all would be different. The child would no longer feel alone and defenceless: the mother – who was not a malicious woman by nature – would have it brought home to her how much her words were affecting her older daughter. Everything that happened from that point would now be different because of the different attitudes and levels of understanding of the characters depicted there. Fran was to continue to allow this 'film' to play in her imagination, incorporating all the sights and sounds of life which would make it more real.

The Fran I first met almost apologized for being there. She spoke quietly, head lowered, as if she did not believe she had anything worth saying. After re-writing this earlier 'screenplay' and imagining the outcome had things been different, she was able to convince her subconscious that she was, in fact, a worthwhile person with a great deal to contribute to life and that she could not allow herself to continue to be influenced by the unthinking words of her mother some time ago.

This was not the end of Fran's problems, of course. We still had to go on from that point to work with Hypnothink to help her overcome various difficulties she was experiencing in her life. The difference was, however, that she could do this with an Inner Face which told her that she was capable and worthy of being helped.

Couples

One of the relationships in life which can possibly give the greatest potential long-term joy is also the one which seems to be fraught with problems. This is, of course, the relationship between a loving couple.

If the self-image of one partner is lower than it should be, the relationship is never going to be entirely happy. The opportunity will always exist for one person to dominate the other – even if they do not set out with the intention of doing so.

Not only is it disheartening to feel that you are being dominated – which, in fact, lowers the self-esteem still further – but it can be exceedingly irritating to live with someone who allows you to dominate them. As this irritability grows, even the more confident partner begins to dislike him or herself for giving in to it.

Mandy and Paul were attracted to each other from the very beginning. They met at work but discovered that they also had many outside interests in common. Paul had recently returned from working in New Zealand, while for Mandy this was the first relationship she had been involved in since the break-up of her engagement some months earlier.

In the beginning all went well and after about six

months the couple decided to live together in Paul's town house. It was only when they were together on a permanent basis that Paul realized how Mandy always agreed with him and always gave way in an argument. She seemed incapable of forming an opinion of her own. If they were going to a restaurant and Paul asked her what type of food she fancied, Mandy would always say 'Whatever you want.' If they decided to have a day out on a sunny Sunday, Mandy would never proffer an opinion as to where they should go but would insist on leaving the decision to Paul.

At first Paul found it quite enjoyable having everything his own way, but he was not really a selfish person at heart and, anyway, he would have liked to do something for Mandy that would please her – if only he could have found out what this would be. He began to grow quite irritated at having to make every single decision and began to play little 'games' with Mandy to see if he could get her to voice an opinion. He would, for example, suggest that they went to an Indian restaurant and, when she agreed, would say that perhaps he would prefer Italian. Once again Mandy would agree and so he would suggest bringing home a Chinese take-away meal instead. Of course, Mandy agreed again.

Paul did not like himself for acting in this way but Mandy's complete compliance with his every wish, every suggestion and every opinion was becoming more and more infuriating. Soon he began to blame her for *making* him behave so badly. She, of course, did not know what she had done wrong and, terrified of losing him, went out of her way to be even more amenable.

It was at Paul's suggestion that he and Mandy came to see me. He really loved her and was unhappy with the way the relationship was deteriorating. For her part, Mandy agreed to this suggestion just as she agreed to everything else. She sat there amazed as Paul tried, as gently as possible, to explain to me what the problem was.

Mandy had not had the happiest of childhoods. Her

father had left the family when she was just three years old and she had heard and seen nothing of him since that time. Her mother loved Mandy and her older brother, but having been left with nothing, was compelled to work full-time and had little time to spend with her children. Her brother Nick used to make fun of her and tease her so much that the little girl used to go out of her way to agree with all his suggestions, just to avoid his bullying.

It was not surprising, therefore, that Mandy's self-image had never been very great in the first place. The one man she should have been able to trust above all others – her father – had deserted her. The next 'man' in her life – her brother – had constantly belittled her.

As she grew older, the fact that, Mandy could understand that her father's leaving had not been a personal rejection of *her* and that the teasing she had suffered at Nick's hands was not uncommon between brother and sister, made no difference at all. These things had joined to form her Inner Face and that, as we have already seen, has nothing at all to do with logic.

It was not surprising that, after such a beginning, Mandy found it difficult to form relationships with boys. Somewhere deep in her subconscious was the feeling that, whatever she did, they would never think highly of her and would probably leave her in the end. So, even when a relationship seemed to begin well, Mandy was always looking for the banana skin – and if she did not find one, she would create it. And each time a relationship came to an end, a little voice in her subconscious mind would say, 'See, I'm right. You're not good enough so everyone always abandons you.' All this, of course, only served to lower her self-image still further.

By the time she met Paul, Mandy's Inner Face convinced her that she would not be able to sustain a relationship by acting as herself. And so, because she had fallen in love and because she was terrified of losing him, she had determined to agree with everything he said and everything he wanted to do. What she had not realized, of course, was that it was this behaviour which was actually driving him away.

It took several sessions of counselling with the aid of Hypnothink to convince Mandy that her self-image was based on a false premise and that she could have – and indeed deserved – the happy, loving relationship she so desired.

Problems with the opposite sex

There are many relationship difficulties with which Hypnothink can help. These range from extreme shyness to dealing with sexual problems.

Mark was a young man of twenty-nine who had never had a serious girlfriend. As a child, Mark had lived with his parents and his three older sisters. His sisters were all outgoing and friendly so the house was always full of noisy, laughing girls.

You might think that, having been used to female company from a very early age, Mark would have no problem at all relating to the opposite sex. But the reverse was the truth. Because his sisters were several years older than he was, they and their friends had always looked on Mark with amusement and good-humoured condescension. This made him shy and awkward in their company and, as he grew older, he did all he could to ensure that he was out of the house whenever his sisters and their friends were present. He joined sports clubs and various organizations where he mixed mostly with other boys.

It wasn't that Mark disliked girls – he just did not know how to act when he was with them. Because of his early experiences, his self-image was of someone who would be teased and ordered around by females – even though his logical mind told him that this would not necessarily be the case with girls of his own age.

As we have seen, the self-image likes to cling on to what it knows rather than go through the awkwardness of making changes. So the adult Mark found himself attracted to dominating women and those who would treat him as someone of little or no importance. So none of his relationships got very far or lasted for long.

By the time he came to see me, Mark had met a girl at work to whom he was attracted – both physically and by her personality. He longed to ask her out but was terrified that, as he put it, he would 'make a mess of it'. Even if he managed to pluck up the courage to arrange a meeting outside work, he did not know what he would say to her.

Mark was able to use several techniques to help him. Firstly he was able to learn to see the past through different eyes so that although he knew what had happened, it could not longer have a detrimental effect on him. Then, using Hypnothink, he worked on visualizing asking the young woman to go out with him. He did not plan a 'script' word for word, but decided roughly what he would say and concentrated on imagining himself being calm, confident and friendly when approaching her.

The next time I saw Mark his emotions were very mixed. He had asked the young woman to go for a drink the following week – and she had accepted. So he was delighted. But now he was beginning to panic as he wondered how he would act when they were out and whether he would do anything which would cause her to make fun of him.

Once again he used the Hypnothink technique to visualize the forthcoming outing and imagine it progressing exactly as he would like it to. Although he had less time in which to practise than on the former occasion, he found it much easier this time – because, of course, he had already proved to himself that the technique worked and was therefore starting out with an expectation of success.

The last time I heard from Mark he had been going out with Suzanne for over a month – and they were getting on famously. I don't know whether the relationship ever became permanent, but it really does not matter from the point of view of Mark's self-esteem. He had successfully proved to himself that he could be taken seriously by a girl and could develop a friendship on an equal footing. He had changed his self-image.

The self-image you form as a result of what happens to you in the early part of your life will govern the way you behave during the rest of it. But that Inner Face never remains the same. If you do not realize what is happening and do nothing to improve the situation, it is going to get worse. Each time something happens because of the Inner Face you already have, the self-image deteriorates a little further.

The wonderful thing is that this does not have to be the case. You have the power and the ability to change your Inner Face – however it may have been created and however long ago that creation took place. All you have to do is make the decision to take that first step.

Just as each failure makes the self-image worse, so each success – however small it may appear to be at the time – will improve it.

Yes, it can be a little frightening to contemplate setting out on a path which is going to make you a different person – but if you are not happy with the way you are now, what have you got to lose?

10

Hypnothink step by step

You have now seen what Hypnothink is, what it can do for you and how you can use it to develop a more positive self-image and thereby improve the rest of your life – as well as helping those around you to make the most of theirs.

Because it is to many people a new concept, the following pages will take you through the entire process one step at a time.

Everyone has a different set of life problems to cope with – a different programming to override – so naturally the precise details of the visual imagery, the affirmations, and so on, will vary. The basic technique, however, remains the same in all cases.

To demonstrate the technique in action, let's refer back to the case of Sandra, who had a horror of water in any form, and see precisely how she managed to completely overcome it.

The details of her case are taken from my own files – although the name, of course, has been changed. But do bear in mind that hers was an extreme case and probably took rather longer to deal with than some other problems might have done.

1. *Know who you are*

Take the time to sit down and discover what you really think of yourself. How have you formed your opinions about yourself – by self-analysis or because you have always accepted the views of other people? What do you like about yourself and what disappoints you?

Sandra didn't just dislike herself – she hated herself! For as long as she could remember she had considered herself inferior to other people. This attitude prevailed in all areas of her life – and not just because of her problem with water, although of course, this only served to make the situation worse.

At first Sandra could not think of any reason why she should have had such a poor self-image as a child. Her parents were kind and loving – if anything they were over-protective. In fact, this was part of the problem.

I explained to Sandra that it was not only harsh or demanding parents who could mis-programme a child, and that even though it was possible that her parents – and especially her mother – had contributed towards her problems, she should not blame them as they were only doing what they considered to be best for their daughter at the time.

When she was very small, Sandra had been quite a sickly child. She had never suffered from a life-threatening condition but she was one of those children who seemed to catch every cold or infection going. This naturally caused her mother some concern – particularly as she was the worrying kind anyway. She did her best to protect her little girl from germs and from conditions which could in any way damage her health. In doing so, she tended to wrap the child in 'cotton wool' so that she did not live the same sort of life as her young contemporaries.

In addition – and without even knowing that she was doing so – Sandra absorbed from her mother a general sense of fearfulness. So, as she grew old enough to make choices and decisions for herself, she continued avoiding what she considered to be potentially harmful situations. At school she would make excuses not to take part in sport or physical education whenever possible and this had the result of causing the other children to mock her so that her sense of being 'different' grew as her self-esteem waned.

One of the things from which her mother tried to protect her was getting caught in the rain or taking part in water sports of any kind. She was always worried that her daughter would get an ear or throat infection and did not think it was worth running the risk. If Sandra ever came in wet after walking home from school, mother would rush to wrap her in towels, rub her hair dry and insist she had a warm bath right away. Little wonder that the girl grew up to think that anything connected with water could harm her.

The adult Sandra who came to consult me was able to see and understand how the problem had started. She did not blame her mother – although she did regret the way she had acted. But now she had decided that the time had come for her to change the situation and put the past into a different perspective.

2. Compile an Inner/Outer Face Profile

Remember that there may be a great difference between (a) the way you see yourself, (b) the way other people see you and (c) the way you *think* other people see you, and that it is only by taking all three into consideration that you can begin to get an image of the real you.

Sandra's Inner Face list looked like this:

Likes:

Kind
Understanding of other people's problems
Hardworking
Friendly

Dislikes:

Stupid
Inferior
Cowardly
Weak
Scared to try anything new
No confidence
Immature

(This list could be shortened by grouping together 'cowardly' and 'weak', and also 'no confidence' and 'scared to try anything new'.)

Now Sandra had to write down how she thought other people saw her. This was her list:

Odd
A misfit
A coward
A loner
Unfriendly

('Odd' and 'a misfit' could be grouped, as could 'unfriendly' and 'a loner' – the list would therefore become shorter.)

When it came to compiling her Outer Face profile, Sandra was faced with the task of finding other people to ask – and then plucking up the courage to ask them. Eventually she selected an older woman who worked in the same office and a girl she had known since her schooldays. Their lists were as follows:

Colleague	*Friend*
Timid	Nervous
Sweet natured	A good friend
Shy	Helpful
Conscientious	Trustworthy
Honest	Fun to be with

Sandra was amazed to read those lists. She had spent so much time thinking only bad things about herself that she had never realized anyone else could think well of her. Even before she started to work with Hypnothink her self-image began to improve. After all, these were people she liked and respected so there must be something in what they said.

3. What do you want to achieve?

Be specific. Don't just tell yourself you want to be 'better'. The more detailed you can be, the easier you will find it to create the appropriate images. And remember to aim high – you deserve it.

In some ways this was an easy question for Sandra to answer – she wanted to react to water in just the same way as everyone else did. But for her it was also such a massive leap from her current position that she found it extremely difficult to contemplate. So we decided to settle for a half-way situation and work towards just being able to run water over her hands. So this was the picture she decided to use when practising Hypnothink.

4. Choose your affirmations

These are the phrases which assume that you have already achieved your goal – the ones you are going to pin up on the wall or keep in your pocket to pull out and read whenever you have a spare moment. Remember that the terminology should always be positive.

Sandra selected three affirmations:

- I enjoy the sensation of water on my hands.
- Water feels good.
- I control the water.

She wrote these phrases on pieces of card which she kept with her at all times, taking every opportunity to look at them. Even though she only glanced at them briefly, it was sufficient for her subconscious mind to be able to absorb the written message.

5. Learn to relax

This is something over which you must take your time. Practise your relaxation technique, with or without the aid of a cassette, over and over again until it becomes second nature so that you eventually reach a stage where you can 'switch off' at will.

This was something Sandra learned to do quite quickly – somewhat to my surprise as she had been so tense when we first met. Her determination to put an end to the problem which had tormented her for so long probably had a great deal to do with this, and she practised several times a day. Within a couple of weeks she had become adept at reaching a deeply relaxed state.

6. Remember past successes

Think back to a moment in your life when you felt the excitement which accompanies achievement. Remember not only what you did but how it felt. Try to recapture that feeling in your imagination. The success does not have to be a great one as long as it was important to you at the time.

This was something Sandra initially found very difficult. Her self-esteem was at such a low ebb that she could not think of anything at all in her life which could be termed a success. None of the usual things seemed to apply in her case – she did not drive, had never ridden a bicycle and (naturally, considering her problem) had never learned to swim. She could not remember ever having won a prize or come top of the class in anything.

We spent some time just chatting about her childhood in general and Sandra talked about her brothers and how they had taught her to roller skate. Also during the course of the conversation she mentioned making the birthday cake for her father and being chosen for the rounders team at school. I pointed out to her that all three of these were achievements at the time. It was the first time she had thought of them in that way but, yes, she did remember feeling proud, excited and elated on each occasion. At last we had found a whole set of positive emotions for Sandra to hold on to.

7. What can you do this week?

Before even beginning to use the Hypnothink technique, find something you can do this week – now – which will set the scene for your future success. Let it be something linked with the achievement you are aiming for and yet something which is within your capabilities.

Sandra decided to go up to the bathroom, turn on the taps at the handbasin and watch the water as it ran down the plughole. She was somewhat nervous about doing even this but overcame her fear by wrapping her hands in a warm, dry towel before turning on the tap, thereby ensuring that no stray drop of water would touch her.

She did this several times a day and, by the end of the week, had become so accustomed to the procedure that the towel was no longer necessary.

8. Create your own 'round room'

Once you are sure you know how to relax, concentrate on creating your own special room in your mind. Remember to start by concentrating on that spot at the centre of the wheel – the one which remains ever motionless. That round room is yours and it is up to you to create the surroundings in which you feel most comfortable. The more you enjoy Hypnothink, the more effective it will be.

Somewhat predictably, Sandra chose a room where the windows were covered by floor-length curtains – where there was no possibility of seeing the rain pouring down outside. She described to me a cosy room with a blazing fire before which stood a huge armchair. This armchair was to be her special place – she would sit in it and feel peaceful, safe and comfortable.

9. *Visualize achieving your goal*

Having created your special place, set aside a time each day to go into it. Most people – particularly those who are new to Hypnothink – seem to find the 'twilight' time between being awake and falling asleep at night the ideal time to choose. Now picture yourself achieving your goal. Just let events happen in your mind. Be as specific as possible. See all the details and allow things to take the time they would take in reality. Really *see* and *feel* what is happening. Be involved. Don't just tell yourself what is going on.

Here Sandra visualized going upstairs to the bathroom, sitting on the stool by the washbasin, turning on the cold tap and letting the water run over her hands.

10. *Link in your feelings of achievement*

While you are visualizing the successful outcome to your chosen situation, remember just how it felt when you were an achiever in the past – even if that achievement had nothing whatever to do with your current goal. What you are trying to do is convince your subconscious mind that you are already someone who is capable of being a success and combine this with the image of the way in which you now want to succeed.

While Sandra was imagining running the cold water over her fingers, she also did her best to recreate the positivity and excitement of keeping up with her brothers when she learned to roller skate.

This part of the process should be repeated as often as necessary until you feel able to perform the previously imagined act confidently and successfully. There is no set amount of time for this to take. Some people will be aware more quickly than others that they are now ready to go and do whatever has been their aim. But even those who are slower – particularly in the initial stages – rarely take longer than three weeks to overcome the first hurdle, and when you consider how long some of them may have been living with their problems, this is really no time at all.

11. Enjoy yourself

Above all – enjoy it! Enjoy the feeling of pleasure and confidence when you picture your own particular happy ending. Take the time to savour that feeling, knowing that you have earned the right to do so.

12. Use negative thoughts to help you

Of course, it would be even better if you managed to keep negative thoughts away altogether, but if they should creep in, see them as a challenge and use your own brain to outwit them. Remember Roseanne who wanted to take her grandchild to the park. If you can't keep negative thoughts away, turn them to your advantage by making them part of the story.

For some people what has been detailed above will be sufficient to help them overcome their entire problem. But for those, like Sandra, whose problems are so deep-rooted and of long standing it may be necessary to work in stages.

Having reached the point where she had no trouble at all in letting water run from the tap over her fingers,

Sandra then went on to work on being outside in the rain. Although this would appear to be the greater step, it was actually easier to achieve than the first stage as Sandra had by then a previous success to build upon. As far as Sandra was concerned, the whole process from initial consultation to being able to walk in a shower of rain took a few days over seven weeks.

There are just a few rules which, if you remember them, will help you along your way:

- Reach for your target with confidence. Don't entertain a single doubt. You can do anything you want to do.
- Never feel guilty about being happy. Remember, happiness creates well-being.
- Put old hurts and former failures behind you – we all have them. Concentrate only on past successes, no matter how small they may have been.
- Remember that tightrope walker and never stagnate. When you have attained your original goal, that's the time to set a new one.
- Think of negative feelings as a challenge rather than trying to overcome them by force of will.
- Enjoy every moment of Hypnothink. Enjoy the preparation and the practising. Derive real pleasure from the knowledge that every moment spent working on Hypnothink and your self-image brings you nearer to being the person you want to be and living the life you choose to live.

And now it is up to you. Believe in yourself and in the power of your mind and you cannot fail. Practise every day acting the part of the new person you wish to be. You *are* that person.

Appendix

Taking things further

Selected reading

Coleman, Dr V. *Mind Over Body*, Guild Publishing, 1989.
Lindenfield, G. *Super Confidence*, Thorsons, 1989.
Robbins, A. *Awaken the Giant Within*, Simon & Schuster, 1992.
Syer, S. and Connolly, C. *Think to Win*, Simon & Schuster. 1991.

Relaxation cassettes

For more information, contact:
The Hypnothink Foundation
PO Box 66
Gloucester
GL2 9YG
Great Britain

Hypnothink training

If you would like details of how to become a Registered Hypnothink Counsellor, please send a stamped addressed envelope to The Hypnothink Foundation at the above address.

Index